CW00642213

How It Happened Here

The Making of a Film

Kevin Brownlow

Introduction by David Robinson

UKA PRESS
Published by UKA Press
UKA Press, 55 Elmsdale Road, Walthamstow, London, E17 6PN, UK
UKA Press Europe, Olympiaweg 102-hs, 1076 XG, Amsterdam, Holland
UKA Press Japan, St.Anders, 108 2-5-22 Shida, Shizuoka, Japan 426

2 4 6 8 10 9 7 5 3

This Edition Copyright © Kevin Brownlow 2007

Kevin Brownlow has asserted his right under the Copyright, Designs and
Patents Act 1988 to be identified as the author of this work

This book is sold subject to the condition that it shall not, by way of
trade or otherwise, be lent, resold, hired out, or otherwise circulated
without the publisher's prior consent in any form of binding or cover
other than that in which it is published and without a similar condition
including this condition being imposed on the subsequent purchaser.

First published in Great Britain in 1968 by Doubleday & Co. Ltd.

A CIP catalogue record of this book is available from the
British Library

ISBN: 1-905796-10-2
978-1-905796-10-6

Printed in the United Kingdom

Without limiting the right under copyright reserved above, no part of this
publication may be reproduced, storied in or introduced into a
retrieval system, or transmitted, in any form, or by any means (elec-
tronic, mechanical, photocopying, recording, or otherwise), without the
prior written permission of both the copyright owner and the
above publisher of this book.

To the memory of

Pauline Murray (1922 - 1994)

and

Miles Halliwell (1931 - 2004)

Contents

Introduction by David Robinson   Page   11

It Happened Here—Credits and Synopsis   Page   21

Author's Preface   Page   25

1   A Primitive Start   Page   29

2   Agonising Reappraisal   Page   41

3   A Second Front   Page   47

4   Where are we going?   Page   57

5   Subsidy and Subsidence   Page   63

6   Porchester Hall   Page   75

7   The Long March   Page   81

8   Applying the Brakes   Page   89

9   Whatever Happened to Your Film?   Page   97

10   Back Into Action   Page   101

11   Ah, Those Radnor Days!   Page   111

12   A Brush With Our Subject   Page   123

13   The Flanders Front   Page   127

14   False Alarm   Page   135

15   The Rest Should Be Easy   Page   139

16   Detained in Hospital   Page   143

17   The Nazis Speak   Page   153

18   Final Surrender   Page   161

19 Picking Up the Pieces   Page 169

20 Festival Time   Page 177

21 The Unkindest Cut   Page 185

Checklist: Kevin Brownlow   Page 197

Checklist: Andrew Mollo   Page 201

Afterword: The View from Forty Years On   Page 205

Acknowledgements   Page 211

How It Happened Here

The film *It Happened Here* is available on DVD from:
Milestone Films,
PO Box 128,
Harrington Park,
New Jersey 07640-0128,
USA.
Phone: 800 603 1104 ~ fax: 201 767 3035
e-mail: info@milestonefilms.com
Web site: http://www.milestonefilms.com

It is also available on VHS (PAL) video from:
The British Film Institute,
21 Stephen Street,
London,
W1T 1LN,
United Kingdom.
Phone: (020) 7255 1444
e-mail: video.films@bfi.org.uk
Web site: http://www.bfi.org.uk

A British edition of the DVD is available
from Film First, Packers House, West Street,
Hereford, HR8 0BX. Phone: 0870 264 9000
Web site: www.moviemail-online.co.uk

Enquiries regarding film rental and public performance
should be addressed to the same organisations

Introduction

David Robinson

Every viewing of *It Happened Here*, I find, requires the same adjustment. You always prepare yourself to make allowances, to be indulgent because, after all, it is only an amateur film, made on half a shoestring—schoolboys' pocket-money virtually—with the barest of technical resources and volunteer personnel who came and went as the shooting stretched on. Yet within the first few minutes, practically within the first few shots, you find that allowances and indulgences are quite misplaced, because what you are seeing is simply a good film at any level and by any standards. As sheer professional filmcraft it is admirable. The staging of the war and the war period have a conviction which eludes more glossy and expensive 'historical' productions. The narrative structure is loose and casual, which makes it all the more remarkable that the film has a dramatic drive which carries through from the first shot to the last.

The credit titles are backed with martial music. Then, over an animated map of the British Isles, the voice of John Snagge sketches in the 'historical' background which is the premise of the film:
'The German invasion of England took place in July 1940 after the British retreat from Dunkirk. Strongly resisted at first, the German army took many months to restore order. But the resistance movement, lacking outside support, was finally crushed. For three years it lay dormant. Collaboration increased as the population became adjusted to the tedium of occupation... Then, in 1944, the resistance movement reappeared ...'
The heroine, Pauline Murray, is one of the population trying to adjust to the circumstances of occupation. She is a district

11

nurse, living in a rural area which the Germans are evacuating in order to root out partisans. A handful of evacuees is left behind. In a skirmish between Germans and partisans, all of them but Pauline are killed. This incident convinces her that the only way to restore life to normal is to support the forces of law and order, whatever they may be. She makes her way to a ruined London and volunteers her services as a nurse. Despite her protestations that she will not do anything political, she discovers that the only way she is permitted to work, the only way of supporting 'law and order' is to join the Immediate Action Organisation. In a London occupied by German troops, she sees the Organisation at work—its strong-arm methods, its violence, its oppression and racism. She discovers, too, its unpopularity with the civilian population through small, veiled insults against her person and her uniform.

The first serious conflict within herself comes when she learns that some pre-war friends, a Hampstead doctor and his wife, are sheltering a wounded partisan. She tries (despite their shock at seeing her uniform) to help them. When they are arrested she falls under suspicion and is posted off to a remote country nursing home.

Here the atmosphere is altogether different: an Edwardian mansion in a summer countryside seemingly untouched by war and occupation. Russian and Polish workers and their families who have contracted tuberculosis are received tenderly and cheerfully by the staff. The children are given toys; they are all put to bed in a bright sunlit ward. Pauline's duty on her first evening is to give them their injections.

She wakes late next morning and hurries on duty to the ward. It is empty. Only then does she understand what sort of injections she gave them.

At last she resists. She is arrested. But the partisans and the Americans are advancing, and she and her escort fall into their hands. Pauline, now classed as a collaborator, is asked to nurse partisan wounded. The last view we have of this war-torn

England that never, mercifully, was, is of a group of partisans who have rounded up a large mass of English collaborators. They shoot them.

The cohesion of all this narrative is especially remarkable when one recalls the lengthy genesis of the film. Kevin Brownlow was 18 and working as a trainee cutter when he had the original idea. In May 1956 he began shooting, kicking off, with typical optimism, with the sequence of a Trafalgar Square rally. On his second day out the camera was stolen. Shortly afterwards he met his co-director, Andrew Mollo, who was then aged 16. The most remarkable instance of Brownlow's steely determination is the revelation of how at this point he junked every inch of material he had shot because it did not satisfy him, and began the whole thing over again.

After two years they were still grinding on, despite defections of crew and cast. After three years they approached the British Film Institute's Experimental Production Fund, and were refused help on the grounds that the film was not experimental and had nothing to teach other film-makers [sic]. After four years they showed their material to Granada Television and were told it was 'crap'. After six years they were turned down by a prospective producer and by the NFFC. And only then did their first break come when Tony Richardson secured them finance to complete the picture on 35 mm. In May 1964, eight years and twenty days after the first shots were made, *It Happened Here* was finished. And then (as Kevin Brownlow describes in this book, with remarkably resilient humour) the real trouble began. By this time he was 26; Andrew Mollo was 24.

One aspect of the whole thing that I find especially intriguing is the change that must have taken place in the boys during this time. People alter and develop a lot between 18 and 26, 16 and 24; how much was the maturing of two unusually lively and responsive adolescents reconciled with the patient compila-

13

tion of a unified creative work like *It Happened Here*? The fact is, of course, that they grew up with the film and within the film, and the film grew with them. *It Happened Here* was their education in more respects than the purely technical one of learning the craft of film-making. Kevin Brownlow's account is disarmingly frank in its examination of their ideas and motives. As boys their attraction to the subject—the war period, of which neither could have any but the most hazy recollection—was naive and superficial: 'Neither of us had yet developed an understanding of National-Socialism; we shared the general horror at their crimes, but were fascinated by the unexplained elements of the Nazi phenomenon. I have never been able to analyse this. Both of us are inordinately squeamish. We cringe at the sight of a hospital uniform. Nazism should have repelled us with its constant reminders of brutality. But mysteries continued to cloud the era. And mystery is a powerful attraction.' Their early days were preoccupied with the pleasures of discovering relics and evidences of the era. Mollo was fascinated by the uniforms; Brownlow, one supposes, by the problems of period re-creation. (His earliest heroes, after all, were the Gance of *Napoléon* and the silent *J'Accuse*, and Maurice Tourneur, the great 'atmosphere' director.)

Work on the film inevitably sharpened moral perception. The story developed as they went along (Brownlow's periodic nagging that they really *ought* to have a script is one of the comic leitmotifs of the book), and with the story a point of view. You detect, in the narrative of the making of the film the stages by which the ethical issues raised by Nazism and racism assumed precedence over the fascination of the purely physical staging. You perceive the difficulties of reconciling the monstrous programmes of British Nazism with the fact that some of the Nazis who helped with the film turned out to be quite amiable chaps in private life (Brownlow clearly found it very hard to suppress a kind of affection for Frank Bennett, who shows himself in the film as an extremist of the most alarmingly irrational kind). Perhaps it was the very fact that the ethical bases of the film were worked out like this, empirically, on the spot, as part of the real-life development of moral and political discernment in the film-makers, that makes their picture, if not a specially profound examination of a human predicament, at least a soundly human one.

The different aspects of their progression show in the film. The neo-documentary reconstruction of an occupied Britain, which was their first idea, is done extraordinarily well. The costumes (washed-out pre-war tweeds and awful headscarves), the uniforms, the cars and buses (with *Picture Post* advertisements on the front), the bookstalls with Nazi-glorifying illustrated magazines, the streets, the typography on leaflets and posters, are all impeccably in period. The writing betrays a keen ear for the contrast between everyday speech and the phrases of official pronouncements: one recalls especially the news commentaries and the C.O.'s passing-out speech at the Fascist training school. There are admirable scenes: the opening sequence in which the grainy visuals and rough sound of the original 16 mm shooting become a positive merit in conveying the half-heard, half-seen confusion of the abandoned refugees; the heroine's arrival in a ruined, almost deserted London; the bravura 'occupation' sequence, in which German soldiers pose for snapshots in front of the Albert Memorial and on the steps of St Paul's and fraternise with girls on back-street doorsteps while a military band marches through Regent's Park; uncannily convincing staged newsreels, one of which includes brilliant fake archive documents of the 1914 Christmas Truce on the Western Front. Their increasing interest in the ethical and social mysteries of Fascism led them to propose a heroine who becomes a Fascist not positively or with malicious intent, but simply through her inclinations to conformism.

When I first saw the film in 1964 I wrote of it: 'Politically, I suppose *It Happened Here* has remained the film of an 18-year-old. There is no question of where the film-makers' sympathies lie; the intention of the film is fervently anti-Fascist. At times, though, one feels that the intention might be a good deal less clear to the unconverted than to those of us who begin with an inbuilt sympathy with the film's message. The main trouble lies in the central character who, both as a dramatic device and as a person, is too negative in conception. She becomes a Fascist out of conformism and convenience; and though this is, eventually, the most effective and the most dangerous manner of political recruitment, it is also undramatic enough, in the event, to make it difficult to argue a point from it. It is a good deal easier to make propaganda (and in the best sense this is the object of *It Happened Here*) out of a more positively motivated hero or villain.

'The same sort of subtlety weakens the irony, which at one level Brownlow and Mollo do so well. The newsreel, lauding Fascist achievement and deploring the war brought about in 1939 by the Jewish warmongers, is a take-off of newsreel propaganda so cleverly handled that it might easily seem credible to an uncritical viewer. And again, when the National-Socialist Party members are invited to voice their own arguments (a passage of *cinéma vérité* whose great curiosity almost makes one forgive its in-appositeness in the context of the rest of the film), they do it with a sincerity and fervour that could obscure for the naïvely unprejudiced the malice and hysteria beneath. In a way the film-makers themselves are seduced. They communicate their own delight in the uniform and military show, in the spectacle of an admirably staged Nazi torchlight funeral. This sort of thing is as insidious as dry rot; history has shown that. This admirably achieved, admirably intentioned film could be hot stuff for an audience with the wrong preconditioning. It *is* an important factor: to an extent the success or failure of the propaganda is tied up with the success of the film.'

Three years and several viewings later I am inclined to credit Brownlow and Mollo with rather more political sophisti-

16

cation than I did then, and to see more positive merits in the conception of their heroine. But events have confirmed that their statement was not sufficiently unequivocal in expression for the less discerning viewer to comprehend it. Shipman and King found the film 'most unpleasant'; Daniel Angel called it 'this Nazi picture'; Charles Cooper, like *The Jewish Chronicle*, found the film anti-Semitic. This book relates how United Artists finally exhibited the film only on the understanding that Brownlow and Mollo would agree to the omission of the entire 6-minute sequence in which a group of British Fascists express racialist and other intolerant beliefs.

Even when one concedes a kind of idiot logic, as well as fervour, in the expression of the Fascist point of view, it is hard to credit that reasonable people could really be swayed by it: at least the film-makers were at every point convinced that by giving both sides a fair hearing, Fascism would condemn itself out of its own mouth. The extent of their miscalculation is forcibly shown by the degree of opposition the film aroused. The number of people who genuinely believed it to be anti-Semitic cannot be discounted. The objections, though genuine, were never, it must be confessed, very solidly grounded or rationally argued. *The Jewish Chronicle*, for instance, which found the film totally objectionable at first viewing, regarded it as perfectly acceptable after the simple omission of the discussion sequence.

The excision of this sequence brings out a rather embarrassing conflict between one's sense of ethical propriety and of artistic correctness. On the one hand one must regard United Artists' decision to cut the film—and to persuade the film-makers into endorsement of the cut—as indefensible. The artist in any field, and the film-maker (as being specially vulnerable) in particular, must be defended against censorship from whatever source. At the same time, from an aesthetic point of view, I do not deeply regret the loss of the passage. I am more convinced than I was in 1964 that it is an excrescence. It is interesting that this sequence and another—the Nazi funeral—having in common that they are the most spectacular and the least essential sections of the film, were both made after the film-makers had finally found a source of finance. God knows one would not wish anyone the privations of the first six years of *It Happened Here*; yet the film may owe not a little of its rigorous quality to the disciplines that poverty imposed.

This is only one of a heap of lessons and precepts and morals about the art and craft and industry of film-making that Brownlow's charming, optimistic, sometimes naive, always witty and singularly readable book enforces. The most substantial lesson they learned, of course, starting as wide-eyed *Amateur Cine World* readers, was about the realities of the commercial cinema, the nature of an art whose means are so costly that it must always, apparently, be controlled by the uncreative. As their concerns bring them more and more in touch with the professional cinema, the heroes and villains become more sharply defined. The uncreative aristocracy of the industry reliably hand out discouragement and disapproval (until, of course, the film makes its own success; and then they come back with their maddening 'Ah, but ifs'—'If I'd been here then...', 'If your new project was as commercial as I.H.H...'). It is the creators who, equally reliably, help them on their way—Tony Richardson, whose role here is angelic; and Stanley Kubrick, who bothers to give them the reel-ends from *Strangelove*. The critics are a funny lot, capriciously handing out praise and damage, hopping about in shameless volte faces to keep abreast of success. But it was Gordon Maithouse, of *Amateur Cine World*, who lent them their first camera (the one that was pinched); and Derek Hill who gave them their first boosts.

I must finally record one peculiar—and on the face of it quite uncritical— personal relationship with the film. No matter how often I see it, I find myself, though I am not particularly emotional, on the point of tears—generally at the most improbable places, like the credit titles. I often have the same experience with the book. I am unreasonably moved by the cool silliness of Kevin Brownlow's decision that since he is earning £4.10s a week and has pocket money as well, it is time that he embarked on a personally financed film; or the impression of Andrew Mollo, as 16-year-old co-director and military historian, perversely spelling 'up' with three p's when corrected for using two. They are not boy wonders, but people. The only other point I can recall in the cinema which produces this absurd tearful effect upon me is (equally improbably) in Leni Riefenstahl's *Olympische Spiele*, towards the end of the marathon, the little dark man (I think he was an American Indian called Brown) who has pistoned along, mile after mile, collapses at last and is swept up into a steward's arms, wrapped in a blanket, the hero reduced to a baby. Here of course the situation is reversed—the babies became heroes—but the conditions are the same: the confrontation of individuals of ordinary frailty and a totally superhuman undertaking. The size of

A German anti-partisan unit drives
through the village of Eashing, Surrey

19

the undertaking, the magnitude of the effort involved in keeping it alive, through eight years during which discouragements and setbacks far outnumbered the strokes of luck (and when anyway the boys had at the same time to be thinking about serious ways of earning their living), *had* to be communicated to the film. I think it is the sense of triumph that makes me cry.

They had to be lunatics, of course, to do it. (I suppose I knew Kevin Brownlow was a lunatic the first time I set eyes on him, maybe eleven years before the appearance of *It Happened Here*. Somebody had dragged me to a house in Hampstead because, they said, it was something worth seeing. I was not convinced it was worth losing Sunday afternoon to visit a skinny little boy in big spectacles who had turned his bedroom into a toy Odeon with tabs and tickets and a single record turntable with which he deftly arranged incidental music to a 9.5 mm projector. Until, that is, the actual film came on and proved to be the earliest restoration of Gance's *Napoléon*, then a lost film, which the child had painstakingly reassembled from reels in 9.5 mm libraries.)

It is the majestic lunacy, though, of the true creator. The danger is that they could be cured of it, brought into a closer but less fruitful accord with reality with the help of people like the Granada man who called their material crap; the Germans who booed; the Jews who called it anti-Semitic; and the *Telegraph*'s man who called it, ironically, 'a weak story'.

Credits: *It Happened Here*

Production Company	Rath Films/Long Distance Films
Producer/Directors	Kevin Brownlow, Andrew Mollo
Script	Kevin Brownlow, Andrew Mollo. Based on an original idea by Kevin Brownlow
Treatment Collaborators	Dinah Brooke, Jonathan Ingrams
Production Assistants	Johanna Roeber, Rosemary Claxton, Alice Brooke-Howard, Graham Samuel, Prince Marshall, Pat Sullivan, Eric Mival
Director of Photography	Peter Suschitzky
Additional Photography	Kevin Brownlow (16mm)

Editor	Kevin Brownlow
Art Director	Andrew Mollo
Military Consultant	Andrew Mollo
Music	Jack Beaver. With excerpts From Bruckner's Ninth Symphony and the German march 'People To Arms'
Sound Editor	George Fisher

Pauline Murray (*Pauline*), Sebastian Shaw (*Dr Fletcher*), Fiona Leland (*Helen Fletcher*), Honor Fehrson (*Honor*), Colonel Percy Binns (*IA Commandant*), Frank Bennett (*IA Political Leader*), Bill Thomas (*IA Group Leader*), Reginald Marsh (*IA Medical Officer*), Rex Collett (*IA NCO*), Nicolette Bernard (*IA Woman Commandant*), Nicholas Moore (*IA Group Leader Moorfield*), Miles Halliwell (*IA Political Lecturer*), Claire Allan and Carol James (*IA Girls*), John Herrington (*Dr Westerman*), Bart Allison (*Skipworth*), Stella Kemball (*Nurse Drayton*), John Snagge, Alvar Liddell, Frank Phillips and Michael Mellinger (*Announcers and Commentators*), Peter Dineley, Frank Gardner, Pat Kearney, Derek Milburn, David Meeker, Michael Passmore, Barrie Pattison, Ronald Phillips, Bertha Russell, Christopher Slaughter, Pat Sullivan, Ralph Wilson, Alfred Ziemen.

Running time: 99 minutes (after cutting of National-Socialist discussion sequence, 93 mins.).

Original Distributors: United Artists (G.B./U.S.). For information on present distributors and availability see Page 10.

Synopsis

It Happened Here tells the story of Pauline Murray, a district nurse, who is evacuated to London because of a resurgence of partisan activity in the South-West. She intends to continue nursing, but finds that the welfare organisations have been placed under overall Fascist control. Realising she has no alternative, she enrols in this Immediate Action Organisation and goes through an intensive training course. She visits an old friend, Dr Richard Fletcher, living with his wife and child in the basement of what was once his house—now requisitioned because of his refusal to join the IA. During a visit to the cinema, Pauline sees a propaganda film showing the German arrival in England, which insists on an ancient friendship between the two countries, and which puts the blame for the war on to the Jews. She soon finds that her IA uniform alienates those around her. When she goes back to the Fletchers, the shock of seeing her in uniform appals her friends, who are hiding a badly-wounded partisan. Discovering the man, she pleads with Fletcher to hand him over to the police. Fletcher reasons with her, explaining that while she despises the partisans (because of her experiences in the South-West) she gives her support to the Fascists. 'And the most appalling thing about Fascism,' he says, 'is that it takes Fascist methods to get rid of it.' Pauline finally realises that the Fletchers need her help, and she tries to obtain morphia from a friend in the IA. The girl attempts to report Pauline, but fails. Before she can return to her friends, Pauline has to attend the funeral of an IA officer, where she experiences the National-Socialist attitude towards the death of a comrade. When she eventually reaches the Fletchers she sees them being dragged out of the house by SS men—together with the wounded partisan. Reprimanded by an IA Commandant for associating with political undesirables, Pauline is transferred to a country hospital. The hospital turns out to be a quiet, almost idyllic place—but oddly empty. Soon, however, a batch of Russian and Polish workers arrive, suffering from TB. All are inoculated. The following day Pauline discovers that the inoculations she has administered have done their intended work. The patients are dead.

Placed under arrest for refusing to carry on, Pauline sits handcuffed to an SS man in a railway carriage, recalling the excuses of the hospital staff. Falling into partisan hands, after an ambush on the train, Pauline is ordered to a field dressing station in a forward area, where the Army of Liberation is staging an offensive. An English SS unit surrenders to the partisans. A scuffle breaks out. The tension snaps, and the shooting begins. Inside the dressing station, Pauline tends the wounded while the radio blares news of partisan successes. From the distance comes the sound of machine-gun fire.

Pat Sullivan and Andrew Mollo prepare detonators for rocket launchers.

Author's Preface (1967)

This story of the making of *It Happened Here* is not presented as an object lesson in film production. Far from it. We made many mistakes, and, as we struggled for finance, the film dragged on for years. Although I have aimed at the truth in telling this story, the whole truth would be impossible, not only for reasons of space, but also because of the risk of libel. Condensing the complications has made the picture sound far easier than it was. It was an unusual subject, and it was unusually difficult. It began as an amateur film on 16 mm; it ended up as a 35 mm production on the screen of the London Pavilion. As the film grew, so the going became tougher.

The knowledge we gained was not entirely beneficial. Many of our illusions were shattered. We learned about the incredible waste of the professional industry. We experienced incompe-

25

tence, indifference and direct sabotage. But there was a positive side to the experience. We learned not only about film-making, but about the historical background to our subject. Most important of all, *It Happened Here* brought us into contact with some remarkable people, and we gained a deep respect for the many who worked with us, who proved once and for all that the cinema cannot be an individual's art.

A title on the picture acknowledges this debt. We cannot name all who helped us; we can only offer them our deepest gratitude. This book, I hope, will return a little of what we owe them.

The Capture: *the German patrol and Eve Markham-Ward*
as a Maupassant heroine

Trafalgar Square, October 1956

*Delay on a London session—a riot squad becalmed in King's Cross.
Christopher Slaughter in foreground.*

28

1: A Primitive Start

To set down the memories of this period is to re-experience them. This I find acutely depressing. The early days of the film were days of despair, and to go through them for the sake of this book will reveal some uncomfortable truths. Over the years, it has been easy to let people think that I was once a minor visionary, taking on a large-scale feature film at the age of eighteen, dragooning friends and passers-by into crowd scenes, staging battles and rallies and causing mayhem in Central London.

Some of these facts are correct, but they suggest a colourful fantasy which does not compare with the truth. When I began this film, I had no idea it would take so long. I was convinced that once I had demonstrated my skill with a few sample sequences, a producer would sign me for some big feature, thereby relieving me of responsibility. The heart of the matter lies in one important fact—there was no script.

My first film, *The Capture*, had been shot without a script, although the story upon which it was based, Guy de Maupassant's *Les Prisonniers*, had acted as a guide. For this new film, I produced a single-page outline, but that was all. Actors, technicians and friends begged me to write something more substantial to help them to understand what I wanted. I refused.

The reason behind this refusal is significant. After *The Capture*, I knew I was capable of making films, but I knew that a script was beyond me. A script required careful thought, deliberation, long hours of unrecognised work and, above all, discipline. If the script was a failure, I would receive no support for the film; I dared not show all my cards at once.

In the past I have explained that the celebrated Trafalgar Square sequence was tackled first because it was the hardest thing to do, that overcoming it would prove the film could be made. This was only partly true. The real reason was more plausible. The Trafalgar Square rally, the whole film at this stage, was sheer adolescent exhibitionism. I allowed my obsession with films to run away with me. Instead of starting at the bottom and working patiently upwards, I intended to begin on the heights, in a blaze of glory.

In 1956, eleven years after the war, London had only just begun to recover. Bombed sites were still visible all over the city. The war was not so much a memory as an integral part of the atmosphere. Everyone over the age of fifteen had been affected by it, and still had clear recollections.

For several months, I had been a trainee in the cutting rooms of World Wide pictures, a documentary film company based in Soho. Trainee was another word for errand boy; my most frequent duty was to carry cans. I carried cans to the office in Soho Square. I carried them to preview theatres in Wardour Street. And I carried them to Humphries Laboratories, just off Tottenham Court Road. Oddly enough, this was the most enjoyable part of the job. Central London was unfamiliar; it was spring, it was sunny, and these walks provided time for reflection.

After *The Capture*, I was anxious for another project. *The Capture* had taken three years, had involved a cast of nearly a hundred and had hardly been shown at all. The story had been set in the Franco-Prussian war; modernised to 1940 it told how a German patrol, captured by a forester's daughter, is taken into custody by the local National Guard, who are given credit for the whole operation. The story was a study in irony. I weighted it too heavily with drama and detail and lost the delicacy of the original. But the film had been well received, and the encouragement of such people as Lindsay Anderson and Derek Hill stimulated me to ideas of another picture.

Walking towards the laboratories, I was jolted by a black Citroen screeching to a halt. The driver leaped out and ran to a delicatessen. He paused at the door and shouted to his companion in German. The scene was straight out of a war film; only the surroundings were unusual, The incident triggered a train of thought. What *might* have happened if the Germans had invaded England?

From this premise, I worked out the basis for an extravagant piece of historical fiction. The single page outline was entitled, emphatically, *It DID Happen Here!*

'While studying the national characteristics of the English and German, the film will try to demonstrate the inevitability of war, by showing from one side its utter futility, and from the other its invaluable stimulus to the development of the human race.'

The central character was to be a woman, forced to evacuate her home in the country and move to London, the much defended capital of Occupied England. The outline gave details of the background, but avoided the personal story, of which I had only the vaguest ideas. But the hypothesis grew more and more flamboyant, describing how the Germans had broken through to Russia, and were subjecting America, the one strong power holding out against the Axis forces, to heavy air offensives over the Bering Straits. In the West, England, overrun in 1940 and almost completely industrialised, was producing materials to enable the Nazis to rebuild the devastated areas and to establish the New Order even further afield. 'The end of the film shows the woman's final surrender to the Nazi way of life. America realises that England is no longer an ally, even in spirit. Long-range bombers, unable to reach London because of impenetrable defences, drop atom bombs on the Northern industrial towns, crippling the entire country and making it useless to the occupying powers, who move out, as the Romans did in 410, leaving a shattered, degraded population to live together without moral support.'

The manifesto had been written in the first flush of enthusiasm. When I tried to enlarge on it, I found my imagination frozen. The scale of the production, so challenging in the abstract, had become a cold fact.

Those who read the outline asked some uncomfortably leading questions. 'How are you going to stage it? Who will you get for the crowd scenes? What will you use for money?' Finance I regarded as the least important obstacle. I have no head for business, and no talent for fund-raising. I limped through *The Capture* by spacing out the shooting sessions until I could afford them. In those days, I depended upon pocket money, earnings from odd jobs and a series of articles on film collecting which I wrote for *Amateur Cine World*. This series was still running, and I was also earning £4.10s a week as a trainee. I could order film stock at trade rates and on credit. Uniforms and props I could borrow for next to nothing from Peter Dunlop, a costumier friend. Somehow, I would manage...

As an act of encouragement, Gordon Malthouse, the editor of *Amateur Cine World*, lent me his 16 mm camera and on Sunday, 6 May 1956, without attempting to secure permission, I invaded the May Day Rally. By mingling actors dressed as German soldiers among the people in Trafalgar Square, I thought I would obtain a spectacular crowd scene.

The leading actor, playing a German naval officer, sauntered into the square in search of the leading actress—who had yet to be cast. A Nazi eagle flaring from his jacket, he was followed by three German soldiers, one of them carrying a Schmeisser sub-machine-gun, the other two clutching rifles. To my relief, no one took the slightest notice. It was the hottest day of the year, and the crowds had come more to sun themselves than to listen to speeches. Unfortunately, they were gaily dressed and wreathed in smiles. No one looked sullen or cowed or in any way under duress, which was more than could be said for my extras.

A group of Danish girls watched our antics. 'We knew this was a demonstration,' said one, 'but we didn't know it was a Nazi demonstration.' When one person notices you filming in a crowd, the message is transmitted with telepathic speed. 'Take off those jackboots!' yelled a voice from the balustrade above our heads, 'Take off those caps! Go on, take 'em off! We'll have no aping of Fascists here.'

A policeman arrived with a Party representative, who accused us of posing the soldiers in front of the banners. We were given no alternative; we had to go.

The Trafalgar Square sequence would have to be reshot, but after our May Day escapade, would the Ministry of Works grant permission?

The police, alerted by the sight of German uniforms, pursued the unit from the location to their cutting room base. An incident from 1956.

'What exactly do you wish to film in the Square?' asked a Ministry official.

'A scene with some soldiers.'

'Soldiers? How many soldiers?'

'About ten,' I lied.

'I see. Will you be bringing any heavy equipment, lights, generators?'

'No, nothing like that. It will all be very simple.'

'Very well, Mr. Brownlow, I see no problem...'

And in due course a little card arrived from the Ministry giving permission for a session between 8 and 10 a.m. on Sunday.

Setting up a session, even at this primitive stage, required an incredible number of telephone calls. From the list of actors and technicians, I selected the people we required. Some of them were only too anxious to help. Others, dismayed at the prospect of getting up early on a Sunday morning, presented innumerable excuses. Most of the calls had to be made during working hours, and I was guiltily aware that I was paid to work as a trainee, not to squander my time on private errands. If this session was a success I could relax for a while, and concentrate on my job. Until then, the film came first.

There was something terribly wrong with the Trafalgar Square sequence, and as the precious film whirred through the camera, I felt slightly sick. The extras were stiff and self-conscious, and the props and costumes hung limply, soaked by the spray from the fountains. I could manage none of the subtler forms of direction; all I could do was issue instructions and get the cast moving, like a traffic cop.

The failure of this vital scene hurt. During the next few sessions, several actors walked out, including the lead. Faced with a growing pile of material, practically all of it useless, and a growing pile of debts, I should have seriously considered abandoning the project. For some reason this never entered my head. Setbacks had occurred en masse during *The Capture*, yet the quality of material had been more imaginative and more satisfactory. Strongly influenced by silent films, *The Capture* depended upon pastoral effects and careful lighting to create atmosphere. *It Happened Here* was largely an exterior picture, and the quality of photography was dictated by the weather. So far, both had been dull.

One evening, I met my art director, Jim Nicolson, to discuss plans. He had agitated for a script since he joined the unit. How could he design a scene he knew nothing about? I avoided the issue, and began discussing the Trafalgar Square session. Nicolson analysed its faults, and drew on a piece of paper an indication of what it *should* have been.

He placed the long banner, with the inscription DEUTSCHLAND UND ENGLAND — EINE RASSEGEMEINSCHAFT! (Germany and England—One Race!) on the dais, and positioned ten flags behind it. The central point was a huge swastika. It was a bold design but I was very dejected.

'Why couldn't we have thought of that *then*?'

'We can still do it,' said Nicolson.

'Again?'

'It wouldn't cost that much. We've got four of the flags. We've got the banner, and we've got the swastika for the dais. But we need more people than we've had before. And you must get better uniforms.'

'What's wrong with the ones I've got?'

'They're all right for long shots, or for close-ups if your photography is rough. If your photography is sharp and clear, it will show up all the defects.'

I decided that we needed a technical adviser. One of the volunteers who wrote in after an appeal in *Amateur Cine World* was a former sergeant in the Wehrmacht, Franz März, who claimed to have won the Iron Cross first class on the Russian Front, and produced documents to substantiate his story. He was not too happy in England, and seized upon my film as a chance to relive the old days. For the ex-sergeant this was a last chance to be an officer, and he eagerly accepted the post of technical adviser.

To secure Trafalgar Square, all I had to do was to renew the existing permit. Most of the old guard, who had been with the film since its inception, promised to attend. And a number of new people signed on, including an 18-year-old amateur cine enthusiast, Christopher Slaughter, who became the only person to survive the entire picture. We were the same age, and we grimly compared birthdays every time we met, unable to believe that so much time had passed.

The evening before the great day, ITV's news department rang up; they wanted to send a camera crew. Delighted at the prospect of such publicity, I telephoned Nicolson to tell him the good news.

'If they come, I don't,' he said flatly.

I could scarcely believe my ears. How could anything be cancelled as late as this? 'That's your problem,' said Nicolson. 'I work in television. I'm a professional art director. If they find me working on amateur films, it could damage my career. You'll have to put them off.'

Alarmed at the prospect of a complete fiasco, I persuaded the TV people to cancel the call, and told Nicolson he need worry no longer.

'I'm still not coming,' he said. 'I've thought it over, and frankly, I've had enough.'

'But what about the material for the set?'

'You'll have to forget it.'

Realising my plight, my mother broke her rule of non-interference and took the 'phone. Her gentle persuasion was more effective than my protests, and soon Nicolson was having dinner with us. The atmosphere was strained. Nicolson stood by his decision. His livelihood was at stake; why should he jeopardise it? However, he agreed to release the props, but I would have to pick them up—and there were too many for one vehicle.

He lived in Streatham. I lived in Swiss Cottage and could not drive. Furthermore, it was getting late. By one of those unlikely chances which occurred throughout the film, the doorbell rang—and there was a young man called Peter West, offering his services. He could drive. A friend in the police force loaned his car and Franz März agreed to take his vehicle down to Streatham first thing in the morning. I hardly slept that night. At 5.30 a.m. the telephone rang. März was in trouble. He reported thick fog all over London, and he had lost his way. I gave him Nicolson's number and told him to keep trying.

The fog was slightly thinner in the centre of town. An Inspector was on duty with two constables, ready to stop the proceedings unless I could produce my permit. I brought out the Ministry's little card. 'If it was up to me,' said the Inspector, 'you wouldn't set foot on the Square.'

At 8.10, two cars, laden with material for the set, triumphantly raced into the Square. In the leading car sat Jim Nicolson: 'I decided to come after all.' While he supervised the construction, I took over a cul-de-sac behind the Square and put the fifty extras into uniform. Residents, disturbed by the commotion, must have been startled by the sight that greeted them. Grouped around an open car, which was used as a clothes-store, a number of men were undressing in broad daylight. Steel helmets and swastika armbands could hardly have allayed their bewilderment. Fortunately, the actors looked too sheepish to cause real alarm.

When the set had been erected and the actors positioned, the result exceeded my hopes. Nicolson had done a splendid job. But filmically, how could I do justice to the scene? I had not learned how to appraise a set from the camera point of view. I settled for a straightforward long shot, with a few close-ups. The establishing shot was framed by the heads of some extras standing in front of the camera; this gave the impression of a crowd.

A nagging suspicion of mediocrity haunted me as I watched the set being dismantled. Suddenly I spotted a perfect set-up: three-quarters on to the plinth, with a Landseer lion dominant. This should have been the main establishing shot. Our cameraman had used his own equipment on this session, and I had left the camera loaned by *ACW*'s editor in the open car. To my horror, I discovered that the man detailed to guard it had wandered off to watch the shooting—and the camera had been stolen.

The following morning, the press broke the story of our 'Nazi Rally'. The *Daily Mail* headlined their pictures: 'The Nazis Are Here in a Boy's Film!' The *Express* countered with a follow-up story the next day, which quoted the Ministry of Works: 'It was due to a complete misunderstanding on our part. We do not allow filming in costume in Trafalgar Square. Had we known it was going to be in Nazi uniforms we should not have granted permission. This is probably the first time anything like this has taken place there—and the last.'

Right — *Andrew Mollo's costume department, 1957*

An encounter on a deserted army camp

2: Agonising Reappraisal

As the winter of 1956 took its grip, and the chance of people agreeing to get up early receded, I gloomily took stock of the situation. I had spent money I did not possess, lost several friendships and squandered the leisure of people who could ill afford to be deprived of it. Before this, I could have abandoned the film at any time. Now I was committed to finishing it—not only for my sake, but for theirs. But the sad truth was that *It Happened Here* had advanced only fractionally. The number of shooting days had been few, but the amount of stock exposed had been disproportionately high. Publicity, however, had been widespread, and many volunteers had written in. German war souvenirs continued to trickle through the post. An *Arbeitsdienst* flag arrived from a public library in Penge, a Gauleiter's hat from a source in Hornsey. There was a good supply of glistening medals, gaudy armbands and colourful badges. Completely unobtainable were boots, tunics and caps. Wartime souvenir hunters, like magpies, picked out the prettiest items.

However, I was told of a Russian family in Kensington who collected old helmets, and someone reported that a stall in Portobello Road market specialised in military uniforms, particularly German. I went to the market and discovered a small booth, lined with helmets, swords, flags and medals. My first impression, of a military cornucopia, was misleading; there was precious little of any practical use.

'I'm looking for German uniforms,' I explained to the stall-holder. 'Do you have any tunics or peaked caps?'

'There's very little about. I've got a lot of collectors on my books. They're all after it.'

'Can you put me in touch with some of them?'

'Well, there's one.'

He introduced me to a young man who looked like an art

student. Forewarned about collectors, and believing the newspaper line that they were all raving Nazis, I regarded this one with suspicion.

His name was Andrew Mollo and he was, in fact, an art student. He said he was very interested in collecting German military uniforms, and actually owned a number of items.

I decided to impart my secret in the hope of eliciting further information. 'Did you know,' I said, 'that there's a Russian family in Kensington who collect old helmets?'

'I think that's us,' said Mollo diffidently. His family specialised in military history. I told him about the film, and the idea excited him.

'Why don't you come and see my collection?' he asked. Never appear too eager with collectors: being a film collector myself, I was well aware of this golden rule, so I waited a few days.

The first surprise was his house, an imposing Victorian building in Queen's Gate Gardens, Kensington, the sort of place used by Embassies. And his room was most unusual. Well proportioned, it had a red ceiling, one black wall and two white ones. Art student whims, I surmised. But at the back of my mind was a disturbing recollection: red, white and black were the German colours. A bust of Hitler, standing on a bookcase, alarmed me further.

My anxiety was overwhelmed by enthusiasm when I caught sight of a field-grey German peaked cap. I had searched everywhere for one of those. Mollo also produced a soldier's tunic, in perfect condition.

'Would you consider helping us on the film?' I asked. 'If you allowed us to use your uniforms, we would give you ours.' My collection consisted of some bric-à-brac, one heavily patched Wehrmacht tunic and some made-up uniforms. Mollo agreed: 'I'd like to put my collection to a creative use.' He added that he had been collecting for about a year.

'How old are you?'

'Sixteen,' he said.

Sixteen! To an eighteen-year-old, sixteen is not merely young, it is infantile. Several boys had asked to help on the film, but had drifted away after the first few sessions. In this case, time would tell.

Andrew was eager to see what had so far been shot, so I asked him round to my parents' flat, set up my projector and screened the rushes on the wall. I had no illusions about the material. I thought it adequate, and no more. But Andrew was bitterly disappointed. To him, a film was a film—something you saw at the cinema. He had never heard of amateur films. He thought *It Happened Here* was a full-scale, professional production. Even his untrained eye could see that the material was bad.

'It's all incorrect,' he declared.

'What's incorrect about it?'

'Everything. Nothing's right.'

Offended, I diverted his attention from the film and produced the prize of my costume department, a German officer's tunic.

'That's incorrect, too.'

'That,' I informed him, 'is absolutely authentic.'

'Excuse me,' he answered aggressively. 'The collar patch is wrong. The pockets are the wrong shape. The badge is made up. The whole thing is a costumier's invention.'

For one awful moment, I thought he was going to back out. I didn't mind losing him—he would obviously become an embarrassment, anyway—but I had to hold on to his tunic and hat. I later discovered that Andrew was not the sort of person to throw up his hands in despair. Instead of thinking 'How can I get out of this?' he tried to work out the best way to improve the film.

One answer was to discard all the old material, and re-shoot it with the correct uniforms. We had lost several actors, so a certain amount of re-shooting was essential. But we could hardly do the Trafalgar Square scene again, and there was a sequence including German aircraft, shot at a Battle of Britain display, which could never be repeated. Andrew said he was willing to involve himself completely in the production. He would ensure that the uniforms and equipment were absolutely correct. But he did not want the effect ruined by the early material.

'All right,' I said. 'We'll redo the scene building up to the rally just as soon as we have enough uniforms.'

Andrew rapidly acquired a number of rare items; a black SS tunic... an army greatcoat... soldiers' tunics... As he became more involved with the project, he introduced me to his family. His father, Eugene Mollo, was Russian. His mother was English, a brilliant photographer and portrait painter. The oldest brother, John, was an illustrator and collector, and he and another brother, Boris, collected English military equipment. Andrew's father specialised in Russian Imperial items. At this period, Eugene Mollo sharply influenced my approach to the film. His philosophical discussions were often hilarious, but always profound. They gave me a groundwork in political history, and made me acutely aware of my ignorance on the subject. Eugene Mollo's detached analyses, tinged with cynicism, helped to mature *It Happened Here* from an action melodrama to a political investigation.

Andrew himself, although only sixteen, gave an impression of confidence and self-reliance which belied his age. He was still rather inarticulate, and his struggles to express himself often made him furious. But before long he was a powerful ally, possessing the all-important business acumen which I lacked.

He was also very practical; his talents embraced sculpture and textile design, as well as drawing, carpentry and costume, though he disliked writing, and spelled 'up' with two 'p's'. If you pointed this out, he would spell it with three 'p's'. This stubborn individuality made him totally unpredictable. I could never forecast how he would react to a particular idea or situat-

Their first session together: Andrew Mollo and Kevin Brownlow, with (centre) *Peter West.*

ion, and this made the reaction all the more interesting. Andrew was obviously an ideal technical adviser. But Franz März still filled this post and I knew that any attempt to remove him would arouse the Teutonic Furies.

So I marked time, trying to think of a solution. The solution was provided by März himself a few weeks later, when he decided to emigrate to India.

Gradually, members of the unit departed, to be replaced by fresh talent; Grant Thomson, from Vogue studios, an enthusiastic actor and cameraman until he went abroad; and Rosemary Claxton, a colleague of Grant's from Vogue, who became stills photographer and continuity girl. She later started a department

45

for civilian wardrobe and tracked down authentic clothes of the 1940s period. The presence of people like this on the unit gave me a new impetus.

For our first session together, we had an ideal location, littered with war debris, an original Mercedes car and accurate uniforms. But these elements were not enough. My approach was wrong. I was reproducing, against a real backdrop, a totally unreal scene—a scene from a war film instead of an incident from life. To add to my difficulties, I was having to photograph it myself. The cameraman from our previous sessions was not available, and since our regular camera had been stolen, I was forced to hire one. The machine was unfamiliar, and its complicated gadgetry alarmed me.

While coping with the actors, I often resorted to uninhibited bullying, not through malice but simply to disguise my lack of confidence. There are no worse ways of directing people than shouting at them. I was aware of this, and tried to remain calm. I would explain a scene carefully and then watch a rehearsal. If the scene looked poor I would lose my temper—not with the actors but with my inability to get the scene right. Andrew and I yelled angrily at each other. Neither of us knew exactly what we wanted, but we both knew it wasn't this.

The rushes were depressingly bad. Even Grant Thomson, the optimist of the unit, complained. That evening, I decided to call a halt. The seeds of discontent sown by Andrew had at last taken root. We would start again. The previous months would have to be written off against experience.

3: A Second Front

The chance of beginning again is available in all the other arts. Paper or canvas can be thrown away and the cost is measured only in tears and effort. For film-makers, however, a fresh start is an almost unknown phenomenon. Too much is at stake in terms of time and money for a film to be discarded and re-shot—an act which, in professional circles, is regarded as the ultimate in failure. But this was my picture. The decision was mine. And I knew I could not live with what had so far been shot.

The fresh start is on a par with confession. You unload your anxieties and misdeeds, have the slate wiped clean, and take a deep breath. The past is forgotten and forgiven. But there is no absolution without repentance. Before starting again on *It Happened Here*, I had to prove that the past had really passed. From a drawer, I lifted out every can of negative bar the Trafalgar Square session. I opened the cans and tipped the negative into the wastepaper basket. Some of the film unwound and filled the basket with glistening, writhing celluloid. I stamped on it and crushed it.

Instead of virtuous satisfaction, this irrevocable gesture left me feeling sick. All that time, all that money, all that effort. What if there was something worth keeping? Perhaps I was only trying to conceal my blunders, as an unsuccessful surgeon buries his mistakes. In case these blunders should fade from my memory, I retained the 16 mm print as an awful warning.

Now that the film was to begin again, I decided to do something about the lamentable state of our public relations. The cast had been told nothing in the four weeks since our last session. I wrote the first of a series of unit bulletins, entitled 'To Put You in the Picture', explaining the delays, appealing for more extras, more uniforms and equipment, and even advertising for financial support. But personal contact was by far the most effective method of enrolling actors. We extended our recruiting drive to include the National Film Theatre; as audiences came out, we thrust enrolment forms into their hands like street corner evangelists. I remember spotting a man in an underground train with a face ideal for an SS officer. I followed him off the train, stopped him on the platform, and persuaded him to join the cast.

Andrew and I talked constantly about the film. Although we didn't know it then, the problem we were trying to solve was that of style. What pictorial form should the film take? Andrew supplied the first clue when he acquired a book called *A Paris, Sous les Bottes des Nazis*. This rare edition, published by the French Liberation Forces, consisted of press pictures and private snapshots, all of which powerfully created the atmosphere of occupation. At first, I was blind to the importance of the book. My ideas were still firmly planted in movies, and I looked at the pictures with a purely academic interest. But Andrew kept referring to them: 'That's what the film should look like.' I examined them again and gradually, whenever I thought about scenes for the film, I saw images from these photographs. Why were the stills from *It Happened Here* so different?

The first thing I noticed was the part played by light. Our scenes had been photographed in dull, grey weather. These pictures had been taken in a variety of conditions: a lone German cyclist, silhouetted against an empty street, wet from a summer shower... soldiers strolling with their girlfriends in the sunshine, their field-grey uniforms uncomfortably heavy against the cotton dresses of their companions... a German sergeant in a greatcoat and peaked cap walking past a horse and cab, the wet pavement reflecting the glimmer of the gaslamps. The way the light gleamed on steel helmets, the way peaked caps threw eyes into shadow, the way the sun conjured textures from flat surfaces—for the first time I began to appraise the pictorial value of light.

48

Then I noticed the importance of the background. In all these pictures, there were characteristic details surrounding the main subject. It might be a propaganda poster, a German signboard, the blurred shape of a passing truck. However indistinct, the shapes lent an indefinable atmosphere to the scene, marking it as authentic.

These photographs had captured not just the location, but the feeling of that location at that period.

As a military historian, Andrew was intuitively aware of the elements which produced authenticity. But intuition cannot easily be communicated. In these early days of our partnership, we argued over everything. These arguments were often bitter, but they forced us to support our opinions with facts, and we both learned a great deal.

We learned most about the Nazi era. The arrival of parcels from French or German collectors aroused a sort of archaeolog-

ist's excitement in both of us, for we were piecing together the history of a dead epoch. The Nazi era was as forbidden a subject at that time as pornography to the Victorians. Neither of us had yet developed an understanding of National Socialism; we shared the general horror at their crimes, but were fascinated by the un-explained elements of the Nazi phenomenon. I have never been able to analyse this. Both of us are inordinately squeamish. We cringe at the sight of a hospital uniform. Nazism should have repelled us with its constant reminders of brutality. But mysteries continued to cloud the era. And mystery is a powerful attraction.

Almost accidentally, we discovered whole chapters of history we knew nothing about. What was this triangular patch on the sleeve of an SS tunic? It proved to be the insignia of the Dutch Nazi Party. We found the handbook of the Dutch Nazis, 1942 issue, and the foldout photographs of mass rallies suggested that the official apologia for collaboration as 'a few hundred discontented Dutchmen' was something of a distortion.

As the costume department increased, so the possibilities of making an absolutely authentic film seemed less dreamlike. Andrew managed to conjure rare items from thin air. The only disadvantage of this sleight of hand was its cost. Our parents steered clear of our financial entanglements, and our slender earning power could not keep pace with expenditure.

As we worked towards the first session of the new film, we held special photographic evenings, which served both as casting sessions and as a reference service. A dozen names were chosen from the cast list, Andrew fitted them in newly-acquired uniforms, and Rosemary photographed them. The results enabled us to see what the actors looked like in black-and-white— they often looked like different people—and allowed us to select the best faces.

Left — The uniforms had to be scrupulously accurate—and equal care had to be taken with casting

51

We soon realised that however authentic a uniform, it will not look right unless worn properly. Some people—I am one of them—look ridiculous in uniform. Others assume a new character.

Comparing these posed photographs with the pictures in the Paris book taught me the final truth: the difference lay not only in the authenticity of uniform and background, but in the physical attitude of the people in the picture. The soldiers in the Paris book were soldiers. Ours were pretending to be. The difference stood out even to the untrained eye.

When people become camera-conscious, a strange force takes hold of them. Their faces assume expressions of pain. They hold themselves stiffly, uncomfortably. The first task of a director dealing with non-professionals is to break through this barrier of self-consciousness. It can only be done by making the scene seem real to those taking part. When we realised this simple fact, it changed the style of our film.

Several amateur film-makers had written in response to our appeal in *ACW*, but most of them wanted help on *their* films. Could we lend them uniforms, equipment? But one letter was unusually interesting. An amateur was planning a film in Canterbury; he was hiring German uniforms and weapons and suggested we come down and take advantage of them. I considered this very generous, but Andrew disagreed: 'His uniforms will be the usual costumier's rubbish,' he said. 'What he really wants are ours.'

Nevertheless, I arranged a meeting with this film-maker, who turned out to be little older than we were. He was working in an advertising agency, and he planned to spend his holiday making his film on 8 mm. It was to be set in France during the Normandy Invasion. I asked him how many troops he planned to use.

'Oh, it's not that kind of film,' he said. 'There will be a few scenes at headquarters, After that the boy is on his own. There will be no one else. I just want to see if I can make a film about someone doing nothing for twenty minutes.' I shuddered at the thought.

'No battle scenes, no invasion scenes?'

'No, nothing like that,' he said, eyebrows rising. He offered his help on our picture, and I added his name to the cast list: Peter Watkins, Capel, Surrey.

The session was getting ominously close. We planned to shoot background material for the rally, so I turned to the Paris book for inspiration. Many of the photographs featured white wooden signboards, direction pointers for military transport drivers. We decided to reproduce these in London. It's easy enough to make such a decision, but another thing to put it into

The session at St. Martin-in-the-Fields

53

practice. The signboards could not be attached to walls without causing damage. We could not dig holes in the pavement for posts. Andrew therefore made a concrete base, supporting a wooden post, to which the signboards were nailed. While he hammered planks, I carefully imitated the German style of lettering. I began ambitiously with such marathons as NSKK TRANSPORTGRUPPE TODT and GENERAL DER LUFTWAFFE LONDON, but the lettering took an incredibly long time. I quickly lowered my sights to more modest announcements, such as GL/514.

But the main attraction of the session was a German army Volkswagen jeep. Andrew had spotted this vehicle in the Cromwell Road; it belonged to a garage, who hired it out to us

The officer with the cigar had delivered the sermon a few minutes earlier. Centre: *Richard Golding, film-maker*

and allowed us to spray it field-grey. We took a gamble on the weather: the paint was water-paint and a shower would remove it.

Fifty extras arrived, not one of them right for the part of a German officer. 'See if you can find one,' I said to Andrew, pointing to the crowded pavements. It was a Sunday, and the congregation was just leaving St Martin-in-the-Fields. Within a few moments, he had found a tall, blond, Germanic-looking man, ideal for the part. Bewildered, the man allowed himself to be fitted into uniform and placed in the jeep. We explained what the film was about, and he relaxed. He pulled out a cigar and, conscious of the gaze of the crowd, began to enjoy himself. 'Don't let the vicar see me,' he said. 'I'm an evangelist. I've just delivered the sermon.'

What a difference the set-dressing made! A grey, huddled mass of civilians clambered out of the truck. A soldier with a rifle stood by as an NCO checked the number, and reported to an officer; it was a simple shot, but it fascinated me. I added little bits of background action, altered the timing, and tried it again and again. The mind plays tricks with the film-maker. The scene may be satisfactory, but how can he be sure? There may be a fault with the camera. There might be something wrong with the action that he didn't notice. With all the money and effort that has gone into the setting up of the scene, it seems foolish not to take it again... and again. Time and energy are recklessly consumed in a quest for perfection which, when the rushes come in, usually proves futile. Take one was all right all the time.

I was setting up for some close-ups when a police sergeant produced his instructions concerning our activities. We should have left at 9 o'clock, and it was now 10. No permission had been granted for the use of German numberplates. One of our vehicles was parked on a zebra crossing, and we were in the wrong location, anyway. 'You said you'd be working in St Martin's Lane. This is St Martin's Place.'

55

A dreadful misunderstanding, I pleaded. Could he allow us to finish? We would take no more than half an hour. After a pause, he announced that he would take the responsibility on his own shoulders. My childlike faith in the police force did not allow me to recognise the implication of that remark: I was convinced that to tip policemen was illegal as well as distasteful. The sergeant, however, went as far as he could without actually submitting an invoice. When we had finished, he came up again. 'I hope everything was all right,' he said.

'Yes, yes, yes, and *thank you*,' I said, effusively.

'You realise I had to take responsibility—just in case anything happened...'

'Yes, yes, yes, and *thank you!*'

'We try to give as much help as we can.'

I discovered later that the tactful way of showing gratitude is to offer a note or two 'for the Police Athletic Fund'.

As the unit lorry drove back to Queen's Gate Gardens, Andrew and I sat among the equipment at the back. 'Well,' he said, 'if they all go like that, it'll be easy.' I foresaw the irony of that remark, even then. But for the first time since I began *It Happened Here* I was elated. Not only had the session gone like clockwork, the scene itself had looked excellent. Suddenly, I remembered it was my birthday, and I sobered down. I was already nineteen. We *must* get a move on and finish the film.

4: Where Are We Going?

The most impressive and moving amateur film I have ever seen was made by a country doctor, whose remote practice on the Welsh border formed the background for his film. Entitled *Driftwood* and *Seashell*, it recorded the progress of a painting from the inspiration to the final result. What made the film extraordinary was the way in which its maker, Richard Jobson, had captured his interest and enthusiasm. More than that, the film conveyed his personality, his philosophy and his feelings towards his painting and the countryside around his home. Particularly touching were the few references in the endearing, rambling commentary to his wife. The film enchanted me. I now realise that without it, we might never have completed *It Happened Here*.

Driftwood and *Seashell* won an *ACW* Ten Best award. Derek Hill encouraged the Grasshopper Group to award it their first trophy, and Dr Jobson and his wife came to London to receive it. When the presentation was over, Derek introduced me to the doctor. He, too, was a keen film collector. 'Some day,' he said, 'you must come up and see my collection.'

Afterwards, Derek asked what I had thought of Pauline.

'Who?'

'Mrs Jobson…'

'I never met her.'

'What a pity. I thought she'd be ideal for your film.'

There was still no sign of a leading lady, although I had interviewed several possibilities, including one well-known actress. We aimed at shooting as much as we could without her.

The police allowed us only two-hour bursts on Sunday mornings. The most hazardous aspect of this fragmented shooting was that sunshine one Sunday would be followed by a downpour the next. Since the scenes had to be intercut, this ca-

Richard and Pauline Jobson

used me some anxiety.

Following the St Martin's session, we staged two more short scenes at a location adjoining Admiralty Arch. At the first of these, we had some friendly policemen from Cannon Row station. Whenever we needed to boost our crowd, they gently manoeuvred bystanders in front of the camera.

Assisting Andrew as technical adviser on this session was Guntis Zarins, formerly of the Latvian legion of the Waffen-SS.

A German officer was played by a German tourist, and his uniform attracted the attention of a number of bystanders.

One of them came up to the officer and pointed to his revolver holster. 'You should wear that on the other side. I was in U-boats, so I know.'

Another tourist approached. 'He should wear it at the back. When I was in the Luftwaffe, we wore it at the back.'

Yet another tourist, a former Wehrmacht man, moved the holster to another position. Finally, Guntis Zarins ambled over. 'It is correct where it is,' he said. 'I was in the SS. I know.' The other veterans retained a respectful silence. Shooting stopped in August: three sessions of two hours each. At this rate, *It Happened Here* would take a lifetime.

Working in the cutting rooms, I had easy access to 16 mm equipment, and although the rally scene was incomplete, I exp-

Trafalgar Square

erimented with editing. One cut sorely troubled me. A mid-shot showed a Blackshirt approaching a German policeman; the policeman was facing left. The reverse angle was a mid-shot over the policeman's right shoulder. The two shots would not cut together. Something jarred. One of the editors at World Wide saw me struggling with the cut.

'You've broken the eyeline rule,' she said.

'The what?'

She explained one of the basic rules of film-making: 'If you're shooting the progress of a car, that car must be travelling in one direction. Therefore, you take all your shots from one side of the road. If you take a shot from the opposite side, the car would appear to be going in the opposite direction.

'It's the same with people. Draw an imaginary line through

the character in the direction he is facing, and keep your camera to one side of that line. If one person is talking to another, then one must face left, the other right. If both faced left, it would look as though they were talking to a third person, whom we never see.'

This eyeline rule may seem obvious, but it is surprisingly difficult. Many directors know nothing about it and offend against it in every film—as does John Ford, who knows about the rule but doesn't give a damn.

I also learned the importance of overlaps. A cut on action makes a smooth transition, but you cannot cut on action without overlaps. If you want to follow a mid-shot of a man approaching a car, to a close-up of him inside it, then you must provide an overlap. The man must get into the car twice—once for the mid-shot, once for the close-up. The editor can then make an imperceptible cut during the action. I also realised how easy it is to listen to advice, and how difficult it is to retain it. You cannot learn how to make films unless you try for yourself.

I took a break from *It Happened Here* and spent a weekend with Dr Jobson in Wales. Wales attracted me not only because of Dr Jobson's film collection. A friend had recently stayed there and had reported a ruined farmhouse, ideal for blowing up. Dr Jobson picked me up from Hereford Station. As we drove the twenty-six miles to New Radnor, the scenery became more and more incredible. Moorland... forest... mountains... striking shades of brown, yellow and green mingled with the orange glow of the setting sun. New Radnor was a paradise the development corporations had somehow overlooked.

The Jobsons lived in a Queen Anne house, set in its own grounds. The living-room was lined with Dr Jobson's paintings, including the one that had inspired *Driftwood*. A room upstairs was packed with film and projectors of all gauges. There was a 35 mm projector in the surgery. I felt completely at home.

Pauline Jobson did not strike me immediately as an ideal leading lady. For one thing she was Irish, and I had always planned the part for an Englishwoman. And anyway, she lived too far away

Another figure who was to play an important part in *It Happened Here* was Mark Dineley, owner of Bapty & Co., the weapon agency. I had hired Mauser rifles from Bapty's when I was making *The Capture*, and I knew Mr Dineley slightly. Andrew knew him better, and one evening he invited him to dinner at Queen's Gate Gardens. We showed him the stills, explaining what we were trying to do with the film.

'You can do some of your battle scenes on my land in Wiltshire,' he said. 'I have a farm you can blow up. My tenant only pays £300 a year for it... he won't mind.'

Mark Dineley was one of the richest characters I have ever met; not merely financially, but as a personality. He was a true eccentric, with a sense of humour which guaranteed helpless laughter from the moment you met him. Bearded, bespectacled, resembling Ferdinand of Bulgaria, he habitually dressed in old clothes, stained with snuff. One eye had been blown off course when, in his youth, he experimented with gunpowder. He was always complaining of approaching senility—'I'm nearly sixty'—but in fact he was extremely tough and resilient. During the war, he had trained the local Home Guard, equipping them from his private collection. His detachment was the only unit to be kitted out with World War One German equipment.

The Priory, at Berwick St John, was Mr Dineley's 15th-century house, full of antiques and rare weapons. It was surrounded by beautiful countryside, as quietly civilised as Radnor's was wild. Flanking each corner of the grounds were heavy cannon. 'Aimed at the church tower,' explained Mr Dineley.

On a hillside nearby was a stone chapel, erected by a local dignitary during the 19th century. Inside were stacks of rifles, line upon line of machine-guns, light artillery, Howitzers, antitank guns... Armoured cars were stored in cattle-sheds nearby. Mr Dineley's offer of co-operation was the most encouraging thing that had happened to us. With all this at our disposal, we could do anything.

We settled on the first weekend in October as the date for the battle session, and a bulletin was despatched to the most reliable members of the cast. 'To be convincing we must have a sizeable proportion of German types on this battle scene. But they must be prepared to rough it. Mr Mark Dineley—who, by putting his collection of German weapons at our disposal, has made these scenes possible—suggests that those actors coming down by car should park them in his courtyard and sleep in them, and that those arriving by train should bring camp beds or sleeping bags and sleep in the weapon store.' We advised actors to bring food to last the weekend, old clothes and plenty of blankets.

Friday night, 3 October 1957. Laden with camera equipment, film stock and tape recorder, I rushed out of the cutting rooms and raced to Waterloo, with minutes to spare for the Salisbury train. Andrew met me, with kitbags full of uniforms. We loaded them into the guard's van and began a journey which changed our lives.

5: Subsidy and Subsidence

Up to now, the film had been shot in short, simple sessions. We had nibbled at it, discreetly, on Sunday mornings. People arrived, they posed, and they departed in time for lunch: they had no time to become absorbed in what they were doing. The first battle session was a baptism of fire. Our status changed from amateurs, quietly amusing ourselves when the fancy took us, to film-makers.

The soldiers on the session, most of whom had been in one army or another, not only had to play soldiers, they had to *be* soldiers. They had to sleep in their uniforms. They had to eat out of their mess tins, drink from their waterbottles. The session was permeated with an atmosphere we had never before experienced. As though by some psychic phenomenon, the little village was transformed into a base for German troops in the 1940s. Everywhere you looked were German infantrymen, German equipment, German vehicles. As the convoy formed up to take the cast and unit to the hilltop location, an old lady passed by with her dog. The dog ran forward and jumped into one of the trucks. The old lady tried to retrieve it, then she noticed the steel-helmeted soldiers. 'You're not real, are you?' she asked.

The battle scene was scripted to take this basic form: a convoy of troops arrives at a lonely hilltop, partisan activity having been reported. The officers examine a distant farmhouse through field-glasses. Nothing stirs. The troops become restless. 'Well,' says one of the officers, 'let's just see what happens.' The mortar opens fire. The farmhouse is struck, but there is no movement from within. The troops move across the open field. Suddenly, a soldier stumbles on a shoe-mine and is blown to pieces. The machine-gun rakes the farmhouse, phosphorus provides smoke cover and the troops charge the farmhouse.

Hans-Joachim Schmittel with Alfred Ziemen, and (right)
Alfred Ziemen in the Hitler Youth, 1943

One or two partisans manage to escape. Another appears with his hands raised, ready to surrender. A soldier throws a grenade and it lands at his feet with a metallic clang. Thoroughly frightened, the partisan screams abuse at the Germans and kicks the grenade away. It explodes as his foot touches it. The troops move forward. Other partisans are routed from their hiding place and shot, and the building is thoroughly searched. The soldiers pull out their dead, tend their wounded and slump, exhausted, round the farmyard. Their vehicles move forward, pick them up and drive on to the next engagement, leaving the dead bodies shrouded with camouflage sheets.

The idea was to show the sort of thing the Germans faced in many occupied countries. We were anxious to depict the German soldier as a human being, not a melodramatic monster. Brutality inflicted by anonymous thugs affects only the stomach. We hoped to affect the emotions. We wanted the audience to feel as if they had taken part in the action, and hoped they

64

would respond to the pointlessness of it all.

Accustomed to two-hour sessions, I looked upon a weekend as an ocean of time, and expected to complete the entire sequence at one go. Having written a rough script for the sequence, I was surprised when circumstances failed to coincide with what I had written. 'Military convoy arrives at hilltop' said the script. Unfortunately we had no convoy. Mr Dineley's armoured cars were out of commission. One of our unit, Pat Sullivan, had offered us a Volkswagen jeep, a German aircraft and a BMW motor-cycle, but to this session he could bring only the motor-cycle. Instead of abandoning the scene, and postponing it for another weekend, I stubbornly clung to the script. I shot from a moving vehicle, as though the convoy was pulling up, intending to do the establishing shot later. This was a mistake. The camera car swayed and bumped at the slightest provocation and much time was wasted trying to get a steady shot.

More time was lost when the German machine-gun failed. It fired a few rounds, and jammed. One of the Germans, who had used the weapon during the Fall of Berlin, endeavoured to find the fault, but without success. Eventually, a vehicle was sent back two miles to the Priory and a replacement brought up. One burst of machine-gun fire, aimed at a grass bank, came perilously close to a group of horsewomen, out for the afternoon. 'I pass here every Saturday,' said one, 'and I always see the military.'

I used a hand-held camera at this session, mainly because Andrew forgot to bring the tripod. These scenes had to be as authentic as newsreels, but I didn't want them looking like newsreels, which to me were synonymous with bad camera operating and jump cuts. (When we came to make a fake newsreel for the film, I made a point of highlighting these defects.)

It was fascinating to see how those who had served in the British army returned from the location, threw off their helmets and equipment, opened their collars, and went off to the pub..

The ex-German soldiers, however, replaced their helmets with peaked caps, brushed off the mud, spruced themselves up and *then* went to the pub.

That night, in the candle-lit draughty chapel, sleep for most of the cast was fitful. Jim Joslyn, the machine-gunner, claimed that two rats sat on his camp bed all night. The two Germans playing officers sought quarters more befitting their rank and booked into a hotel at Shaftesbury. They arrived wearing Wehrmacht uniforms and carrying their Schmeisser sub-machine-guns, and the manager called the police. Since neither of the men spoke fluent English, the police were unwilling to believe their explanation that they were acting in a film.

By the end of the weekend, I had shot the unprecedented amount of 1,100 feet—thirty minutes—and the sequence was only half complete. The only shot which had been really sensational was one in which Andrew, playing an infantryman, was blown up by a shoe-mine. With the rest of it I felt dissatisfied. The sinking feeling in the pit of my stomach was the feeling of failure. Could we afford another of these sessions? When the rushes came in, my suspicions were confirmed. 'There's nothing wrong with them,' said Andrew. 'And there's nothing right with them, either.'

Mr Dineley, as exhausted as we were by the rigours of the weekend, was visibly shaken when we mentioned extra shooting. He imagined that everything had been fitted into the two days. Since his vehicles had failed to work, we reminded him that the convoy, at least, was outstanding. However, we knew that we couldn't afford another session for months. A huge bill for 16 mm stock loomed over my conscience at World Wide. We decided to go out and find finance, instead of waiting for finance to come to us. But on New Year's Eve, 1957, our problems faded. As we saw the New Year in at Queen's Gate Gardens, Mr Dineley made a memorable declaration: 'I think we'll be able to find some money for *It Happened Here*. We ought to be able to subsidise it through the company. We can certainly manage £100 to start with.'

This, we thought, was the beginning of a new chapter. With this money, we would consolidate our resources and perhaps finish the film by the end of 1958. We would both be under twenty-one, with a feature film to our credit; we would have no trouble directing professionally after that. Perhaps we could make our next picture with the same unit? We had several members who were as good as any professionals.

We decided that our first duty was to complete the battle scene. But we could do nothing until the leaves returned to the trees, otherwise the countryside would change from summer to winter in a single cut. A long-range weather forecast suggested that early March often brought spring-like conditions. We arranged to return to Berwick on the first weekend in March. Meanwhile, our film had to take second place to another; I was now a fully-fledged assistant (£11 per week) and World Wide were producing a film about the Trans-Antarctic expedition. Roll after roll of Kodachrome poured into the cutting room, to be screened, logged and assembled. I had no time to think about anything else.

Working as a professional was less of an advantage than I expected. You learned how to handle film as an assistant—you were shown how to join it, you were shown how to rewind it. But no one told you how to cut, or how to direct. There was no training scheme in the industry. Occasionally, someone would ask your opinion of a sequence, or would demonstrate their theories. But few technicians had the ability to teach. You had to make your own mistakes.

Following pages — *The shoe-mine explosion: all that is visible of Andrew Mollo is his rifle*

67

The weapon store provided ice-cold accommodation

Pat Sullivan braves a grenade blast

Following pages — *The extras lived like soldiers and quickly began to look like soldiers*

6: Porchester Hall

During the gap between sessions, my political awareness was roused by a series of lunchtime arguments. My opponent was a young Communist. He accused me of indulging in Fascism for its glamour, and in war for its excitement. My struggles to justify *It Happened Here* as something more than just a war film were partly responsible for it becoming more than just a war film. There is nothing easier than to defend a film that hasn't been made, and as I was challenged, so I invented sequences to fit my argument. Gradually, the film took shape.

'One thing the film *will* be,' I promised him, 'is unprejudiced. I oppose Fascism as much as you do, but I am simply going to present the facts in the film and allow the audience to make up its own mind.'

This enraged him. 'How can you call yourself an artist?' he shouted. 'An artist has to be prejudiced. That is the very basis of his existence.' I was shaken, and realised he was right. An artist has to take the standpoint of his conscience. Yet I sincerely believed in the value of objectivity.

In early March, 1958, Andrew and I attended a meeting at Porchester Hall addressed by Sir Oswald Mosley. I felt a curious mixture of alarm and excitement at seeing authentic Fascists lining the walls, tough stewards with lightning-flash lapel badges, ready to eject hecklers. I recalled reports of Mosley's huge indoor meeting at Olympia in 1934, when Sir Oswald paused at each interruption, searchlights focused on the poor heckler, and the stewards pounced on him, dragged him outside and beat him up. Sir Oswald's matinee-idol appearance had mellowed into stout old age, but he was still a gripping speaker.

Mosley denied that he had anything against the Jews; he pleaded for a United Europe, and an Africa in which blacks would be contained within a solid border of whites. 'But,' he added, 'we would not use force to move those Africans who did not want to move.'

When it came to question time, neither Andrew nor I could restrain ourselves. 'You say you no longer oppose the Jews,' I said. (There was a commotion behind me.) 'In that case how do you justify this?' I held up a copy of *Action*, Mosley's publication, its banner headline attacking some Jewish financier.

Sir Oswald stepped to the front of the stage and held up his hand to quiet the commotion.

'I have never opposed Jews for being Jews,' he said. The hall fell about in merriment. 'I have never been anti-Semitic.' The hall was further convulsed. Flashbulbs popped. 'I only opposed certain Jews for what they did—not for what they were.'

Shouted remarks and laughter greeted this statement. Mosley elaborated on the point, then asked for further questions. Andrew stood up. 'You say you want the Africans to move to the centre of Africa, but that you would not use force. How would you do it?'

'We would merely withhold from them the right to work.'

'Isn't that the same thing? You are forcing them to move.'

Sir Oswald became suddenly angry. 'What do you know about the African situation?' Andrew tried to speak. 'Sit down,' snapped Mosley. 'You've already asked your question.'

A few weeks later, when I was filming an early meeting of the British National-Socialist Movement (then known ambiguously as the National Labour Party), one of the speakers approached me with a gleam of recognition in his eye. 'I know you,' he said, 'you're the one that asked a pro-Jewish question at Porchester Hall.'

I hope he enjoyed the irony, years later, when our film was attacked for being anti-Semitic.

This direct contact with Fascism, peripheral though it was, gave new impetus to the political content of the film. Mosley was no longer just a name in the history books, but a real person we had encountered face to face. Some of his lieutenants had broken away from the Union Movement, dismayed at his apparent abandonment of Fascism, and had formed extremist groups of their own. The press blew this into a Great Nazi Scare, and aided by some pictures of a small scuffle in Trafalgar Square, splashed NAZI RIOT! across the front pages. Most of the reports at this time were sensational nonsense, but the germ of a Nazi revival *had* taken root. We had seen it for ourselves, at street corner meetings all over London. It provided an unexpected and alarming topicality for our film.

Following pages — *Fascist street-corner meeting, 1936, reconstructed in Camden Town. The Mosley figure on the truck is Barrie Pattison, film journalist; Tom Redburn's magnificent Foden steam wagon in background.*

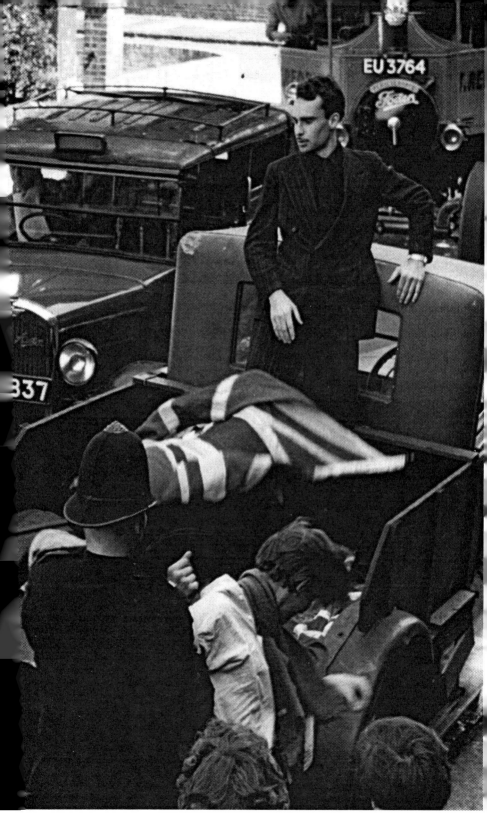

7: The Long March

No one could say that we didn't learn from our mistakes. For the following weekend's battle session we hired a coach to transport the actors and to accommodate them overnight. We warned everyone that the weather was liable to be cold. We arranged for the coach to be parked in Trafalgar Square, the assembly point. A few yards away, another member of the unit manned a telephone box, the number of which was issued to every extra. What could possibly go wrong?

The long-range weather forecast was wrong for a start. There was no sign of spring. The trees were bare, and the weather was icy. The coach crawled into Berwick St John two hours late, having battled through blizzards to reach us. On the hilltop the wind sliced through the thin uniforms. There was no snow, fortunately, and we shot the mortar sequence. But an hour later with a mere 80 feet in the can—it happened.

The first flurry came in horizontally, like interference on a television set. Blown on the teeth of the wind it stung the face like hail. The shooting was postponed. Shivering, the soldiers packed up and clambered aboard the vehicles. The engines hunted angrily as the wheels fought for a grip on the frozen mud. Soon the snow cut down visibility, obliterating the swastika flags strapped to the bonnets of the German vehicles.

In the village, the tarmac roads were light grey; the snow was gaining a grip. What on earth could we do? The cast could be taken home in the coach, but nothing would be gained from that. Now that they were here, they might as well stay until morning. Bitterly, I added up our expenses—£16 for the coach, £5 for hire of boots, God knows how much for stock, petrol, ammunition, and so on. We had thirty people, all the uniforms and equipment we needed, original German vehicles, 1,500 ft of stock and... snow! After conferring with Andrew and Rosemary, I decided to call the whole thing off while the actors' morale was at a reasonable level. All we could do in the snow would be a few close-ups; that would mean keeping the actors hanging around in the cold. Actors will do anything while they have their enthusiasm. But once that goes, everything goes. We decided to return to London the following morning.

That night was the worst anyone could remember. Some of the soldiers slept on stretchers in the unheated, unlit chapel. Others tried to sleep in the coach, but the driver went off to the next village and took the ignition key with him, thus denying the troops the benefit of the heater.

To our eternal shame, Andrew, Rosemary and I took advantage of the comfort and warmth of the Priory. You cannot expect people to endure hardship for the sake of your project if you refuse to share that hardship with them. The next morning I realised our mistake.

At 5 a.m. the storm had stopped, but the snow had settled everywhere. Through the window I could see some of the soldiers stomping miserably up and down the road. I dressed hurriedly and raced outside. The temperature was well below zero, and I gasped as I left the well-heated house. The soldiers had been pacing around, trying to restore their circulation since 2 a.m. Incredibly, they were still able to joke about it. 'If we were doing this for money,' said Frank Gardner, 'we'd never stand for it.'

Andrew and I held a conference with Pat Sullivan, one of our keenest supporters and a fellow collector—of vehicles and aircraft, as well as uniforms. I was in favour of going on, provided that the snow could be cleared from the front of the farmhouse. Sullivan raced off in his Volkswagen jeep to check the situation—and reported that a miracle had occurred. There was no snow up at the farmhouse! We mobilised the cast, took two oil stoves to keep them alive, and drove to the top of the hill, where the wind was so strong that no snow could settle.

We found cold a most effective spur; no one delayed us, no

one held us up with practical jokes. We worked at such speed that there was no time for breakfast or lunch breaks; the cast grabbed what food they could between takes. I found the low temperature very stimulating, and only felt the cold when I touched the camera with an ungloved hand; the metal seemed to burn the flesh.

I made two important discoveries at this session; one was the value of Dextrosol, the glucose tablets. I found I could keep going for fourteen hours without food on two packets. The second discovery was the fact that I was working intuitively. Before, I had been stuck at the end of each shot without an idea of what I should shoot next. Now I found myself taking the establishing shot, then moving in for close-ups instinctively.

The session went like clockwork. The soldiers moved through the smoke under a hail of Bren-gun fire. I shot this as a series of hand-held tracking shots: soldiers' faces under their helmets, their eyes smarting from the phosphorous smoke, moving steadily forward... the Bren-gun firing straight into the lens as the camera gets nearer and nearer...

The hand-held camera movements were shot on a one-inch lens. This is not a practice advisable for normal production; the slightest jolt is transmitted to the lens and appears on the screen as a blur. But in a battle scene, this is not only acceptable, it is virtually essential. The less steady your camera during scenes of violent action, the more effective the result. (To obtain a smooth hand-held track, a wide-angle lens should be used. The wider the lens, the smoother the track.)

Following pages —
(Top left) *5.30 a.m. Pat Sullivan prepares to take his* Kubelwagen *to the hilltop location—to see if snow will prevent shooting.*
(Bottom left) *the vehicle returns with good news—the location is clear. Andrew Mollo fits wartime headlamp shields, prior to moving off*
(Top right) *The cast vacates the weapon store.*
(Bottom right) *Wehrmacht troops have won control of the farmhouse— now the SS take over. A scene from the deleted battle sequence.*

A German officer (Peter Dineley) hurls grenades into the farmhouse at the height of the battle

At the end of the session, my feeling of exhilaration was marred only by uncertainty about the rushes. However, Andrew seemed pleased, and, equally important, so did Mr Dineley. The morale of the cast was high, and that set the final seal of approval on the session.

Back in London, my conscience troubled me about our spending the night in comfort while subjecting the cast to below-zero temperatures, so I wrote a letter which Rosemary duplicated and sent to each of the extras. We apologised for the conditions but thanked everyone for their inspiring assistance. It was just as well we sent this letter; one extra replied that if he hadn't received it he would never have helped us again.

The rushes were exactly what we'd hoped they would be. The two sessions were cut together and at last we had a battle sequence. It had taken only three days to shoot, although there were some vital pick-up shots of the convoy and explosions before the sequence was complete. But for the first time we had a sequence we could show with neither explanation nor apology.

Mark Dineley, with Christopher Slaughter

8: Applying the Brakes

By a unique combination of circumstances, Andrew and I were able to achieve absolute authenticity. So we set ourselves up as authorities on the subject. An article, under Andrew's name, appeared in an amateur film magazine, advocating this approach to historical reconstruction. We cast our experienced eyes with blasé nonchalance over each new war film, expressing impatience with those which failed to measure up to our exalted standards. (The only film in which we could find nothing to criticise was Stanley Kubrick's masterly *Paths of Glory*.)

During a trip to Paris, we saw the relics of the occupation: bullet holes in the steel shutters and the *pissoirs* along the Seine, memorials to executed partisans, rusting metal notices about aerial bombardment. At the flea market, we saw an ancient Citroën truck, its bonnet protected by a Wehrmacht camouflage groundsheet (which Andrew instantly purchased). From stalls run by military specialists, we acquired tunics, caps and equipment. Recalling our shortage of German boots, I pointed out a pair for sale. They were in a state of advanced deterioration, but they were fairly cheap. Andrew showed no interest, so I bought them. In London I discovered they were not even a pair—they were two left-footed boots of the Franco-Prussian war. I did better with my quest for old films, discovering a stall which specialised in silent films and projectors; among the films were original Nazi 9.5 mm newsreels of the invasion of Russia, released in 1941 for home movie use.

We visited the film-maker I most admired, Abel Gance, the director of the 1927 *Napoléon*; this film, with its breathtakingly adventurous use of the camera, had a very strong influence on my own technique. Gance seemed pleased to hear this, and surprised to find anyone so young interested in the past. I showed him a reel of *Napoléon* I had bought from the flea market; he

89

A German NCO (Werner Ballé) in It Happened Here.
The uniform is original

spent some time squinting through a magnifying glass at the tiny frames. We also showed him the stills of *It Happened Here*. He studied them intently, and enquired about the film in detail. 'An excellent idea,' he said, and we purred.

Returning from France, we spent a weekend in Wales, where the subject of Pauline as leading lady was first broached. Honor Fehrson, a friend of Pauline's from the village, asked what my work in the film industry entailed. I explained about World Wide and the Trans-Antarctic film we were making, and then I mentioned *It Happened Here*.

'Any parts for females?' Honor asked.

'Yes, lots,' I replied. 'We could certainly use you—and I'd

A German NCO (Michael Rennie) in The Battle of the V1 *(1958).*
The uniform was made by a costumier

like Pauline to play the lead.' Pauline laughed the remark off.

'No, really,' I said. 'You've got a perfect 1940 face.'

Later, Dick Jobson said, 'I think Kevin is quite serious. You ought to do it.'

Pauline thought, 'Oh well, it's only an amateur thing. What's the odds?' We were not to hear of this decision, however, for some time.

Bad news awaited us on our return to London. Brent's, our long-suffering laboratory, demanded twenty pounds, or else. To meet this bill, and to supply further publicity, we sent some stills to *Amateur Movie Maker*, companion magazine to *Amateur Cine World*. The editor gave us a centre-spread headlined

The Paris flea market. A Citroën truck with Wehrmacht camouflage ground sheet over bonnet; and Andrew Mollo negotiating for the groundsheet. (Eugene Mollo, centre)

'Life isTough in Brownlow's Army'. The captions were credited to 'Andrew Mollo, Costume Director, and Second Unit Director'. Since the St Martin-in-the-Fields session, Andrew had immersed himself in the film as deeply as I had. But I would not admit this, even to myself. I wanted *It Happened Here* to be my film. I wanted all the plaudits, and even at this early stage we were getting quite a few. Later, I realised that his contributions were so essential that I could no longer hog the limelight. Nevertheless, several people strongly advised me to break the association. 'It will do you no good professionally,' they said. They failed to understand that this was no normal production. It had already spread over years. Enthusiasm cannot last that long unless it is re-generated. Before long, we were making the picture on equal terms, as co-directors.

April 1958. An East German film, *Holiday on Sylt*, came into the news: the British Board of Film Censors banned it because it was 'libellous to a living person'. The living person was the Mayor of Sylt, former SS-Obergruppenfuhrer Reinefarth, who was involved in the crushing of the Warsaw Rising. The film contained a Nazi newsreel—a Deutsche Wochenschau—which opened with the eagle and swastika trademark, showed German troops, happy and smiling, on the Russian Front (to be happy and smiling on that Front in 1944 was quite an achievement), and then depicted how the SS were dealing with the Warsaw Rising. It must have left a very strong impression; nine years later I saw the film again and the opening sequence of *It Happened Here* bears striking similarities.

I decided it was time I scripted at least the opening of the film. I produced a three-page outline, which described how a small Wiltshire village prepared for evacuation. The chief character, Alison Russell, is introduced as she helps some villagers to remove valuables from the church. Convoys race through the village; we follow one of these as it drives to an area of suspected partisan activity. So we lead into the battle scene. When we return to the village, evening is setting in. The villagers are worried. They gather in small groups, discussing the situation. Police clear the street. Another column passes through, a heavier column, and the villagers have to press themselves against the walls. Alison Russell looks at the crates on the vehicles, which are labelled 'Giftgas'. The Germans intend to use gas rockets to flush the partisans from their hideouts. The atmosphere of tension is increased. Night falls, but nobody goes to bed. Firing is heard, first far away, then gradually nearer. Anxiety turns to fear, but at dawn the first batch of tired evacuees is transported away from the village in a police lorry. They drive along the same route as the convoy, but now the villages are empty except for troop emplacements. The lorry passes the shattered farmhouse, the scene of the battle, and eventually reaches the railway station. As the train moves out of the station, we cut to a shell explosion, followed by the heavy battle sequence, which builds up the impression of the countryside being utterly devastated. Then back to the train as it nears London...

What I thought was an easy way out—step-by-step scripting— saddled us with a problem we never completely overca-

Richard Jobson took this picture of Pauline shortly after their marriage

me. When we progressed to a complete scenario, this opening became a burden to the story. For the moment, however, I was delighted just toing on paper.

We arranged a session for early June, 1958, anticipating summer weather. The week before the session there was a transport strike, it poured ceaselessly, and it was bitterly cold. I was resigned to cancellation, but the strike was called off and the weekend was extremely hot. The heat-wave reduced our speed, and to make matters worse, we were shooting extra material for the battle scene and had to light fires to supply smoke. One of the fires spread, the hay in the barn caught fire and we found ourselves fighting a real conflagration...

After this session, Andrew went to Germany with his father; we both hoped he would find vast quantities of equipment and uniforms. Neither of us foresaw how much he would find. At first, the German surplus stores were unwilling to admit they had any Third Reich material. But as soon as Andrew had won their confidence, they became more helpful. One storekeeper took him into the catacombs of the Dusseldorf underground air-raid shelters; behind each door were stacks of uniforms, boots and helmets. Prices were gratifyingly low.

While Andrew was away, I had the valuable experience of doing some work with John Krish. World Wide had been asked by the Ford Motor Company for an off-beat comedy, and John Krish adopted a rewarding method for working out the script. We spent a day walking around London, firing ideas at each other and scribbling the results down on paper. The script was his responsibility; I acted as a sounding board, supplying additions and suggestions. The results were so fruitful that I determined to employ the same method on our script—when we came to write it. Later, I became assistant director on the Ford film, which was called *Bandwagon*; the director was Peter Hopkinson, the producer, from Ford, was Karel Reisz. An assistant director is responsible for the organisation and administration; he has no creative participation at all. I was not anxious to be responsible without being creatively responsible, but the chance of working on such a project was too good to miss.

We shot two more sessions, both very successful, and then Andrew made the decision to go to France, to study at the Sorbonne for one year. *It Happened Here* came to a grinding halt. I wondered whether we would ever get any further.

Pauline Jobson as Pauline Murray, photographed during the Camberwell session

9: Whatever Happened to Your Film?

1958 ended considerably less optimistically than it had begun. Although Mr Dineley had given us invaluable help, the proposed finance did not materialise. The battle sequence had been virtually completed; the shooting time had been a week, but the week, spread over weekends, had consumed more than a year. From France, Andrew wrote to say he had discovered unlimited supplies of German tunics. But where was the money coming from?

Derek Hill suggested that *It Happened Here* could have the backing of the British Film Institute's Experimental Film Fund. Derek made preliminary enquiries. A week later, he rang up in some excitement. 'The BFI have £2,500 left,' he said, 'and they want to blow it on something tremendous. They seem enthusiastic about the idea of *IHH*, but they want to see what you've shot so far.'

I sent over the battle sequence. Two weeks later, John Huntley wrote to say that the BFI were impressed by the sequence. 'However, we feel that the size of the project puts it well outside the range of the Experimental Film Fund and is not the sort of film which falls within the terms of our work. I would therefore like to ask you if you have another shorter, simpler project which the Committee might consider.'

My hopes dashed, I arranged an interview with John Huntley. The interview went well; we were back in the running for the £2,500. The BFI Experimental Film Fund Committee gathered one Monday in March 1959 to discuss their current projects, and they asked me to be present. I met James Quinn, Stanley Reed, John Huntley, and Karel Reisz. They were sympathetic and encouraging, but they expressed misgivings about *It Happened Here*—misgivings which, in retrospect, seem understandable, but at the time were baffling. Cavalcanti, they said, had already made a film with a similar subject (*Went the Day Well?*, a film made during the war, in which a group of parachutists, guarding an English village, turn out to be German). The sequence shown was accomplished, but it did not suggest that our film would be experimental. The production would cost far too much money. It all happened twenty years ago, and lacked topicality.

'Other people who have made films with this money,' said Stanley Reed, 'have got close to the mentality of the people they are dealing with. Can you honestly say you would know how the German would behave when he came here?'

'I couldn't honestly say I would,' I replied, 'because it never happened. But both Andrew and I have done a great deal of research into the subject of occupation, and we have built up an enormous library of books, documents and photographs. I think one can only judge such things by the final results.'

Stanley Reed asked, 'Will your film teach anything to film-makers?'

'I can't answer that,' I said.

'The Experimental Film Fund enables people to make films which are different, films which have an original style and say something new.'

'Do you feel anyone has made a picture like this before?'

'I mean in terms of technique.'

I said I thought originality was very rare. 'A film-maker should be healthily derivative. He should have a receptive mind and adapt already existing techniques to his own style. Individuality is what is important.'

'I agree to a certain extent,' said Stanley Reed, 'but take our past films—*Together*, Karel's films—do you not feel that they used original techniques?'

'Not really,' I said. 'I feel they adapted existing techniques.'

The discussion did little to restore confidence. The committee clearly felt that the film was unsuitable. James Quinn said he thought the whole question of political films was a dangerous one.

'Yes,' agreed Karel Reisz, 'but at least he's making an anti-Fascist film.'

Stanley Reed said he would regard in the same light, and with the same degree of importance, a Fascist who wanted to make a similar film.

'I wouldn't,' said Karel Reisz.

The interview culminated with a decision to grant me twenty-five pounds to do a sequence which would prove my ability with intimate scenes.

I decided to shoot some of the village scenes, but first I had to wait for Andrew to come back from the Sorbonne, then I had to locate a leading character. Already the film was vanishing into pink clouds of nostalgia; it had been so long since our last session that when Pat Sullivan drove down from Oxford, we spent the evening like a couple of veterans, reminiscing about our campaign in Wiltshire.

10: Back into Action

Andrew's return from France was the signal for a trip to Wales. We discussed the future of the film with the Jobsons, and Dick made a memorable pronouncement: 'If you feel Pauline would be right, she'd be quite happy to do it.' At last we had the leading character. But how could she spare the time to travel down to Wiltshire? 'Can't you make use of the village up here?' asked Dick. Mmm... the terrain was not the same, nor was the local style of building. But shooting in Berwick St John had grown more and more difficult; the villagers were not very approachable and Mr Dineley was feeling the strain of our exhausting sessions.

The lonely Welsh farmhouse, Black Yatt, was not an ideal location for a spectacular battle scene. It was too remote. The moors, however, had an air of desolation which could easily be captured on film. We would blow up the building, but we would combine the session with another important scene—the execution by the SS of civilians who have missed the evacuation.

The session was arranged for the weekend of 4 July 1959. New Radnor was 150 miles from London, so we took special care over the arrangements. One vital person was Mr Dineley, whom we needed to blow up Black Yatt. He was not enthusiastic about the idea of travelling so far. What about Peter, his son? Could he do the explosions? He had helped us on all the battle sessions and had played a leading role. No, said Mr Dineley, he could not. It would not be safe. With this unique opportunity of securing the vital destruction scenes for the heavy battle sequence, we had to have the explosions. We raced round to Peter Dineley and discussed the situation. He agreed with us, and said he would talk to his father. We continued the arrangements; a nucleus of our own unit would combine with ex-

That idyllic afternoon; Andrew Mollo on lawn, Peter Watkins wraith-like under the tree, Kevin Brownlow, Derek Hill and Peter Dineley

tras from New Radnor. Dick Jobson introduced us to a patient, Heinz Kreiseler, a former Luftwaffe parachutist. In the area, said Kreiseler, were several other former German PoWs, including an ex-SS NCO. He promised to round them all up. Peter Dineley called to say he had secured his father's approval *and* the explosives—and we were off.

The months of inactivity gave this session an added excitement, yet the weekend was surprisingly leisurely. We were equipped to shoot two short sequences—the explosions and the execution. Anything else would be a dividend. Derek Hill, who had done more than anyone to publicise the film, came up to write a piece for *Amateur Movie Maker*. His article, published under the pseudonym of Paul Zammit, began with an account of the disorganised arrival of the unit cars, two of which ran out of petrol on the Welsh border. Next morning, the preliminaries began; the first problem was to find some sacks of sawdust to put down the craters on top of the explosives.

'We went across the road to the pub for lunch,' wrote Hill. "'I bet Dr Jobson's going mad over there," said the barmaid. "We're the ones who're going mad," said Brownlow. "We need the entire village up at Black Yatt tomorrow. How much is a six-gallon barrel of cider?"

"'I've lived here for thirty years," said a man at the bar, "and I've never been up to Black Yatt yet."

"'Well," said Brownlow, "this is your last chance. We're going to blow it up."'

That afternoon we spent luxuriating in the garden. It was excessively hot, and there was nothing we could do before Sunday's main shooting. Actually, I felt a constant nagging at the back of my mind that there was something we *could* be doing.

Without the existence of a full script, however, there was no easy way of checking. I wandered round the garden, past the garage stacked with sub-machine-guns, rifles, uniforms, helmets… past the vehicles parked outside the gates… listening to the laughter of the unit, sprawled on the lawn. A latent sense of responsibility pricked at my conscience. These people had not come all this way to laze around on the grass. I decided to shoot something—anything—to justify their presence.

Peter Dineley and Andrew were sweating up on the moors, digging interminable craters. I went into the village, rounding up extras from the young men just returning from work. Peter Watkins put them into uniform. When the two hole-diggers returned, we were almost ready. Peter Watkins spread the road with hay, branches, mud, stones, tins, and rubble. 'Make it look as though a convoy's been through,' Andrew said. The extras lined up in the road, and Ben Rayner's Chrysler was made ready as a camera car. Villagers leaned over their gates. 'Don't go over there,' said one small boy to another. 'You'll get killed.'

Andrew came out and inspected the location. The rubble was too carefully placed; Watkins had done an over-meticulous job.

'There's far too much in the street,' said Andrew. 'Drive a car through and blow it to the sides.' The Chrysler sped up and down the street. Andrew supplied a lesson tactlessly, but none the less valuably. If you want something to look real, *make* it real.

The sun's flat light began to spread into a more interesting effect as evening approached. We shot scenes of SS troops sauntering through a smoking village, the sun filtering through the smoke and lighting them from behind. The scene looked very good.

'Later that evening,' wrote Derek Hill, 'Ben Rayner said to Brownlow, "I suppose the film's getting on now."

"'Don't be silly,' said Brownlow, "it's only just started."

"'How much did you shoot this evening?"

"'Two scenes—one hundred feet."

"'But it'll go on for years like this."

"'Well, what's wrong with that?'"

At that moment, in those surroundings, I was perfectly happy for the film to go on for years.

Next morning we were up at 6.30 a.m., but it was some time before we could start. For one thing, Black Yatt was obscured by trees. I could find no set-up which gave a clear view of the farm-house. There was only one answer to that, and it was one which horrified Dick Jobson—cut down the trees. This was a problem which could, and should, have been foreseen earlier.

When we did start, however, technical hitches sparked off irascibility. 'Suddenly flames licked around the farm,' wrote Hill. '"Who set that off?" demanded Brownlow. "Someone said ready," bellowed Mollo. "Well, it wasn't me," said Brownlow. "You'll just have to do it all over again." "There's no more pe-

The halcyon days. Kevin Brownlow at camera,
assistant director Eric Mival with notes

trol," said Mollo. "Very clever, very clever," said Brownlow.
"If you'd just stop flapping and hurry up and film you'd be all
right," returned Mollo.

'Tempers cooled,' wrote Hill. 'The refugees straggled past
the camera, a huddle of old jackets and bundles. Suddenly, the
grins and horseplay were gone. They looked like real refugees.

Each time the camera turned there was a quiet chill. It began
to rain. "Good," said Brownlow, "The refugees'll look really
miserable."

'On the first take of the refugees being mown down, Mollo
shot twice and twenty people fell to the ground. There was a
long delay before the retake. "We'll be dead before you shoot
us," said a small boy. Brownlow moved in for a close shot of

the men firing. The sound seemed ear-splitting. Sheep ran over the hill, and in the far distance Dr Jobson chased after his hysterical Yorkshire terrier. The corpses sat up and waited for their close-ups. "That woman's got modern spectacle frames," said Watkins, suddenly. "Thank heavens you noticed," said Brownlow. "And you—how long have you had that jacket?" "Fifteen years," said a youth. "Good. And hide that duffel coat. There weren't any in civilian use before 1949."

'"Running," said Brownlow. There was a loud boom and a corner of the field shot into the air. Then a long, long silence. '"Where's Andrew?" asked Brownlow. "Andrew! Andrew!" shouted several voices. Suddenly a steel helmet flew into the air from the bushes near the crater and everybody broke into relieved laughter.'

When the cast had been transported back to Radnor, we tried to blow up the farmhouse. The first attempt dislodged bricks, but the supposedly fragile chimney remained firmly in place. Finally, Peter Dineley put a charge on the end of a broomhandle and stuck it up the chimney. B-o-o-m. No change. 'That's the end of the detonators,' said Andrew. 'I'm full of respect for the way the Welsh built their houses.'

The rushes were our best to date, the explosions looked vigorous, and the execution had the right quality of casual brutality. A few days later, we heard that the BFI Experimental Film Fund Committee had decided not to sponsor the film because it was in no way experimental. Well, we would have to creep forward on our own.

Right— *Andrew Mollo played a number of small parts; here with Schmeisser sub-machine gun, he mows down New Radnor villagers*

The onslaught against Black Yatt

11: Ah, Those Radnor Days!

A script was written to cover the first three reels of the picture. We strongly doubted whether our finances would take us beyond that point. The script followed the original outline until the second village sequence, which was turned into a full-scale evacuation. The gas rocket idea was thrown out and the scene showed the overloaded evacuation vehicles departing, leaving Pauline and a few others to face a night alone in the deserted village. The little group becomes aware of partisan activity. A convoy arrives, but the vehicles are German. The villagers are as frightened of the partisans as they are of the Germans, but at least the officer in charge is friendly. The sequence ends with an ambush. The officer is killed, and so are the villagers. Pauline is picked up by a retreating army vehicle, and taken to Salisbury station.

The evacuation scene was our next priority. We needed half a dozen old trucks, masses of old clothes and baggage, and the population of the whole of New Radnor. We made the village look as drab as possible. The street was littered with debris, curtainless windows were covered with strips of brown paper, German sign-boards were nailed on to trees.

For the first time there were no German soldiers to equip, no explosives to set up, no heavy armaments to worry about. This was our first civilian session. It was also the first session to feature Pauline Murray. The name of Alison Russell was abandoned for two reasons: the girl in *Look Back in Anger* was called Alison, and friends of Pauline who appeared in the film could never lose the habit of calling her 'Pauline' in front of the camera. (Murray was Pauline's maiden name.) I was far from confident about entrusting this vital role to Pauline. Tests had shown her to be self-conscious before the camera. But the moment she put on her costume, a 1940 two-piece suit, she be-

111

came the character I had always envisaged.

There was no further question of her being right for the part. Now the question was, would I be able to capture her character on film?

The Jobsons told everyone in the village about the session. Since they had been asked by their local doctor, we hoped that they wouldn't dare stay away. The day of the shooting was overcast, and a heavy mist hung over the street. This was a godsend, because it veiled the high hills that made the village so distinctly Welsh. By eleven o'clock we had only six extras. I was panic-stricken. No amount of camera trickery could make lorries seem overloaded with six people! But the villagers were in church. By twelve o'clock, nearly a hundred people had arrived.

When Rosemary had finished costuming the extras, and Peter Watkins had transformed their well-fed faces with make-up, they both came out to inspect the results. To one woman, Rosemary said happily: 'You look perfect, now. A typical wartime refugee.' An awkward silence followed. For this was one person Rosemary hadn't costumed. She had only just arrived, in her everyday clothes.

Again and again the evacuees clambered aboard the battered transports. Again and again the trucks hurtled round the village, horrifying their passengers with a display of speed the vehicles were never designed for. The children entered into the spirit of the sequence. Several of them tried on gas masks—something we wartime children found difficult at the best of times. When they scrambled aboard the vehicles, they struck up a song, 'The Animals Went to the Fair'. As the last truck disappeared into the mist, the refrain 'what became of the monkey, monkey...?' was very touching.

We completed the evacuation in four hours flat, the swiftest session so far. But when the rushes came back, I was dumbfounded. The laboratory had inflicted a set of fine, wavy scratches, the sort of mark that a wire brush would make.

New Radnor children—always willing assistants

Camera scratches are easy to spot because, however intermittent, they are dead straight. This abrasion had obviously occurred since processing. But we could not abandon the laboratory. Its work in the past had been excellent. It was also the cheapest place in London.

Shortly afterwards, we shot exteriors and interiors for the scene in which Pauline takes the villagers back to her house. I was anxious for a night effect that really looked like night. I under-estimated the exposure and ruined the lot. At first I suspected the grading, and cursed the laboratory for a second blunder. They returned a lighter print, but it was grey and lifeless and contained no more detail. It was definitely my fault.

I reshot the night sequence. This time, I fully exposed the negative and simply asked for a dark print. The results were perfect, justifying our use of negative-positive stock. Many amateurs used reversal, which cost less. But exposure had to be precise, and the cameraman had no margin of error.

December 1959, the end of a decade.

Our continuity girl, Rosemary Claxton, announced that she

114

The evacuation, New Radnor

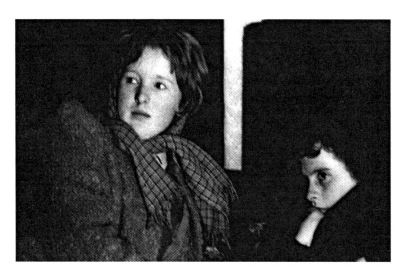

*Left behind after the evacuation, the little group
becomes aware of partisans*

115

was emigrating to Australia. We were sorry to lose her; she had combined the work of stills, civilian wardrobe and general assistant and was thus difficult to replace. Eric Mival, another member of the unit, left for National Service. Alfred Ziemen, our German officer, decided to go to America. Just before he left, we brought him to London to post-synchronise his dialogue. All his shots had been done with a silent camera; we merely kept a written record of his dialogue. Now we made these shots into loops and hired the dubbing theatre at World Wide. Each loop was projected continuously until Alfred had synchronised his line with his mouth movements on the screen. A number of professional actors specialised in this post-synching process, but I wanted to capture Alfred's authentic German accent.

The *Daily Mail* announced a new series, written by C. S. Forester, on what might have happened if England had been invaded. I telephoned the paper and suggested they might like some illustrations. They were not over-enthusiastic; what they really wanted was an impressive poster. Did we have any suitable stills? I thought so—but they didn't. None were dramatic enough, they said. So I arranged a morning session, starting at 6 a.m., for Peter Watkins to shoot stills of SS men against London land-marks. The Mail turned the stills down and used a photograph of Adolf Hitler instead. However, they did print some stills from the film during the series, and paid us fifty guineas. They added £20 for our morning's work, so we were mollified. For the first time we were out of the red.

In sharp contrast to our idyllic New Radnor sessions was a weekend spent on a demolition site at Camberwell. The area looked as though it had been blitzed, and we selected it for Pauline's walk across London. The Friday before I called Pauline to check her arrival time. She sounded very worried. Dick was ill and she couldn't come. It was too late to cancel everything. We decided to go ahead and salvage what we could.

Camberwell children started this fire

The session was a nightmare. Being a weekend, the demolition site attracted children from all over the district. We saw them from the distance, coming in like locusts, a group on bicycles heading the main swarm. Then they were all over us, jumping, tearing, screaming, thumping, yelling. You tore one away from the camera, and six more took his place. They grabbed rifles from the soldiers. They clambered all over the location. Andrew dashed about, retrieving the bits and pieces that had been stolen, and meting out an occasional backhander. I clung desperately to the camera, wondering how long they would keep this up.

Finally herded behind a cordon of troops, they decided to calm down and watch us. Perhaps there would be a battle ? We managed some shots of soldiers flushing refugees from underground cellars. But when no explosions were heard, the children swarmed all over the location again. We were saved from

117

annihilation by the arrival of a middle-aged constable, who controlled them with some good-natured thumps. The children retreated and were ominously quiet until the policeman departed. Then part of the site erupted in thick black smoke. The children, now nowhere to be seen, had set fire to an oil dump. The location began to look like the Russian Front. I swivelled the camera round and pushed the troops towards the fire. Then I ran out of film. In the few minutes it took to reload, the fire brigade arrived and ruined the shot. Police officers also arrived, and questioned us closely. We blamed the children, hoping that might control them. It didn't.

Our wrath was placated by some good news: Dick had recovered sufficiently to enable Pauline to leave. Honor Fehrson drove her to Hereford Station with minutes to spare. In her panic, Pauline left an attaché case, with the costume and gasmask, at the ticket office. As she entered the carriage, she suddenly remembered. 'Oh, God,' she said, 'I forgot my gasmask!' The occupants of the carriage stared at her.

When Pauline arrived, we had to pack two days work into two hours. As usual, Pauline not only entered the atmosphere, she created it. Her appearance among the blitzed buildings, in her 1940 costume, changed the whole feeling of the session. The script required her to look tired, as though she had just stepped off the train after a long, anxious journey—a reaction for which no direction was necessary.

By the time we finished, the children had wrecked everything in sight, and lost interest in the proceedings. The Light Brigade departed, leaving the area clear for the Heavy Brigade—their older brothers. This was the era of flick knives and Teddy Boys. By the time the gang of youths descended, we had packed our equipment into a room of a deserted house. The youths tried to investigate. Andrew guarded the entrance. There was an argument, a scuffle, and some boys grabbed two Mauser rifles and bayonets. They discarded the rifles but ran off with the bayonets. We hastily transferred everything into the vehicles before anything else happened. New Radnor was never like this!

Documentary and feature director Paul Dickson, a few days later, gave me an insight into direction which taught me more than any of these sessions, although I would not have understood unless I had directed actors myself. 'You should try to appeal to the actors' senses,' said Dickson. 'Your direction must get inside them. Take a scene of a woman sitting by a fire. The fire is simply a studio light. There is no atmosphere for the actress to respond to, so you have to provide it with words. Tell her she can smell the burning wood, the faint scent of pine-trees, she can hear the crackling of the logs, she can feel the warmth, the texture of the wool against her skin; gradually, she will respond and give you exactly what you want.'

The following day, Paul Dickson persuaded World Wide to give me a documentary to direct. It was a one-reeler, to be shot in five days flat, a stimulating contrast to my own sprawling epic.

Meanwhile, we returned to New Radnor to shoot the church sequence for the opening of the film. John Leeds, a new assistant at World Wide, took charge of the electrical equipment for the interior lighting. Fascinated with the idea of re-creating daylight with artificial light, I carefully avoided motion picture lighting with its multiple shadows and unreal modelling. Anyone who can handle a camera can handle exteriors; the quality of a cameraman is tested by his interior lighting. I studied the natural effect of the limited amount of daylight, and merely boosted it with the lamps.

The previous night I had been violently ill, but realising that the scene had to be done, I dosed myself and went over to the church. The Bible was open on the lectern at a passage which began: 'And thou shalt have sickness of thy bowels—and thy bowels shall fall out because of this sickness.' Then the Lord wreaked further vengeance. No sooner had I set the tripod up than Andrew tripped over it, and the camera crashed to the gro-

(Above): *the evacuation session,* (Opposite): *the Camberwell session*

und. The back was dented and the motor would not start.

Horrified, I showed the damage to Dick Jobson; he took it home in his car, and returned within the hour, the machine in working order.

The rushes justified all our troubles: the scene looked as though it had been lit by daylight. But when we had to shorten the film for the final cut, this scene was an early casualty.

120

121

Frank Bennett, in SS uniform during the
shooting of the surrender sequence

12: A Brush With Our Subject

21 October 1960: Andrew rang to ask if I wanted to go to a party.

'I hate parties,' I replied. 'You know that.'

'This one sounds different. A fellow called Frank Bennett has just borrowed a Nazi flag. He says he wants it for a party. It's all a bit peculiar, but he's invited us both. Do you want to come?'

Frank Bennett, dressed in a green Tyrolean costume, answered the door. We were the first guests. Andrew's flag hung on one wall. On the pelmet over the curtains Bennett had placed a silver German eagle.

'I'm very interested in your film,' said Bennett. 'I'm also very keen on opera. Now why don't you have a gala performance of *The Merry Widow* in your film, at Covent Garden? I'll play Hitler. We'll have a little blonde girl giving me a bouquet.'

I laughed, but Bennett was serious. As a matter of fact, he *did* look rather like Hitler. He was forty-five, with black hair and a black moustache.

The doorbell rang, and a young man in a long blue raincoat arrived. I glimpsed the badge of the National-Socialist Movement in his lapel. The next guest wore the insignia of Sir Oswald Mosley's Union Movement. Two more guests arrived, saluted the swastika flag, and went over to the gramophone. Instead of dance music, they played the *Horst Wessel*.

The room rapidly filled up with an assortment of the lunatic fringe. Three Hungarian refugees arrived, Nazi badges hanging from their ties like horse-brasses. They explained that they belonged to the Hungarian Arrow Cross Organisation, which was National-Socialist.

'How many of those in the Uprising supported Nazism?' I

asked.

'Oh... ninety per cent.'

It was no use expecting historical truth from this gathering, but some replies to our questions were very revealing.

'Now that I realise what's going on,' I said to Frank Bennett, 'perhaps I could ask you a question. I'm sure you've been asked it time and time again, but I'd be fascinated to hear your answer. How is it, after all we know about Nazism, that you can still support it?'

'What do you mean?' he asked, assuming a baffled air.

'How do you justify concentration camps?'

'Oh... that's simple. In the last war, internment camps were built to house enemies of the state. We had them; ours were on the Isle of Man. The Germans had them, too. Now, the majority of those opposing National-Socialism were, naturally enough, Jews. So more and more Jews were put inside. The internment camps, the concentration camps, began to fill up. Now, the Jews are a filthy race and they brought with them lice and disease. A camp built for 8,000 had, perhaps, 25,000 in it. Disease spread. Now what would you do with 25,000 diseased people? Turn them loose on the population? No; you'd exterminate them. It's the kindest thing to do.'

I was shaken rigid by this reply. I realised that no fictitious dialogue of mine could compete with the real thing. A statement like this reveals more about Nazis, and their state of mind, than any scene of atrocities.

Members of the cast at the local pub, Graham Adam, centre

Ray Wills and Colonel White in the Flanders Truce scene

13: The Flanders Front

A BBC television programme required three extracts. We chose the Trafalgar Square sequence, part of the battle scene and part of our Camberwell shooting. Since the BBC paid expenses, we secured the services of announcer Frank Phillips, one of the best-known voices of the war years. He read the commentary for the Trafalgar Square sequence in one easy take: 'This is London, and these are its people. People with one great and common purpose, to pay tribute to the achievements in their country of National-Socialism.' The commentary, which my World Wide colleague Glyn Jones had written, described how the masses flocked to the Square to give thanks to their Nazi leaders, and it made a startling contrast to the wartime news bulletins Frank Phillips was accustomed to reading. We were apprehensive about his reaction. But as he emerged from the commentator's box, he grinned. 'I've *always* wanted to do that!' he said.

After the programme had gone on the air, the floor manager chatted about our film, and showed us a rare item of equipment—a 1922 hand-cranked 16mm Kodak camera. It is strange how often the conception of an idea is followed by a series of circumstances directly connected with it. Here was an ideal camera for faking early newsreels, exactly what we wanted for our propaganda film.

We would open with the Trafalgar Square sequence, then we would flash back to the Flanders Truce, to show how Englishmen and Germans remained brothers even during the holocaust of the Great War. This was a difficult point to prove, since millions spent years killing millions, but the commentary was suitably ironic: 'Only a handful from either side, but enough to rekindle the flame of comradeship.'

We set up for the 1914 sequence immediately. It was January, 1961: the previous month had brought severe flooding to the West Country. Our location was in Dorset, close to the crisis area.

Although this session dealt with an earlier period than the 1940s, we approached it in the same way. We cast each player carefully, ensuring that he had the right period face. This sort of casting is a neglected art; many period films are ruined because of it. Certain faces are right for certain periods, others are wrong. It is something which has to be judged intuitively: there are no rules. In 1914, most men wore moustaches, so we bought an assortment of false ones. We ensured that all the uniforms were original, and provided the players with Princess Mary's Gift for Soldiers—the royal Christmas present for 1914 was a small tin box, containing cigarettes and sweets. The camera might not pick these up, but they heightened the atmosphere for the soldiers. The combined effect of this sudden switch to World War One, the sight of all the soldiers in Great War uniform, and several sleepless nights during a heavy week resulted in a very strange experience. Without falling asleep, I lay in a shivering trance convinced that I was at the Flanders Front. I remember that someone had dropped his pack with medical supplies somewhere in no man's land, and I had to go out and get it. The rain poured down and I was practically suffocated by mud. The sensation of having lived through the event continued throughout the day. It was extremely cold, and a torrential downpour was whipped into a frenzy by gale force winds. The first person to climb out of his car at the location was Pat Sullivan. His 1914 moustache, stuck with the strongest glue, flew away on the wind. As soon as a camera was erected, the wind blew it into the mud. The rain lashed the lenses, despite desperate attempts to shield them. There was little likelihood of getting anything on film, so I used both the 1922 Kodak and the Bell and Howell 70 DR. Sighting through the viewfinders was impossible—I could scarcely see through my own glasses—so I aimed the cameras like gunsights. My respect for

The Flanders Truce, Christmas 1914, re-created in Dorset for the newsreel-within-the-film. The camera is an original Pathé, 1912.

the old newsreel cameramen increased as I vainly tried to crank the 1922 Kodak at an even speed.

The light grey German greatcoats developed huge patches of damp on their backs; gradually all the uniforms became water-logged and the hats began to wilt. I was wearing five garments, one on top of the other, and was soaked to the skin. Nevertheless, the soldiers whooped and yelled and jumped with enjoyment during the football game, as though they really were enjoying it.

Working on *It Happened Here* had aroused Andrew's interest in motion pictures. He had recently worked on *Saturday Night and Sunday Morning*. Now he started as third assistant director on Tony Richardson's *A Taste of Honey*. This would mean valuable experience for him, but yet another hold-up on production. I wondered whether Andrew would be able to mention our film to Tony Richardson, in the hope of raising finance. He dismissed the idea. 'I'm not going to ask any favours. He gets too much of that sort of thing.'

Instead, I approached Denis Forman, former head of the British Film Institute, now at Granada Television, and offered to show him sections of the film. A screening was arranged, but Denis Forman was detained in Manchester. In his place was a Granada producer.

'It's crap,' he said. 'It's awful. I've never seen such a wasted opportunity. The story's naïve, full of stock situations and lousy amateurs walking around with old clothes that don't fit.'

Coupled with this setback came Andrew's decision to remain with Woodfall for a year. I was fully occupied at World Wide directing my second documentary and editing others.

The most difficult scene in our film-within-a-film was a march-past in Parliament Square. We had already tried it once; we had depended on a single Territorial detachment and only four had turned up instead of the promised fifty. We called upon official assistance, but the Commanding Officer of the Scots Guards was not helpful. 'I'm afraid it would be out of the question for us to supply you with troops,' he said. 'You see, the Panzers have arrived at Castlemartin. You will therefore appreciate that it would be impolitic to march around in Nazi uniforms at this juncture...'

1 October 1961: we tried again, with our own extras and some volunteers from a TA parachute battalion. Cannon Row police promised us no co-operation. The traffic had to keep moving, and we would have to shoot in the gaps. If we caused an obstruction, we would have to go.

A portable speaker broadcast martial music to the troops, in the hope of keeping them in step. Andrew drew up the column of infantry; we had enough for a column of threes. As the band crashed out the opening chords of the *Lippe-Dettmold Marsch*, the column moved forward in perfect step. When our wartime bus, with the *Picture Post* eyes on the front, moved into position, the scene was almost hallucinatory.

Round the corner, sightseeing on their last day in England, were fourteen officers from the Castlemartin Panzer battalion.

Hearing the unmistakable strains of the *Lippe-Dettmold Marsch*, they came into the Square to investigate, and were greeted by a column of Wehrmacht infantry. Astounded, the officers inspected our troops, pronouncing them 'absolutely correct'. They were so fascinated that they insisted on accompanying us to the rest of our day's locations.

Our 1936 street-corner riot was shot in the style of a period newsreel. I instructed Grant Thomson, with a second camera, to stay out of sight while we set up the fight. As soon as he heard it breaking out, he was to come round the corner and grab whatever he could. Meanwhile, I positioned myself on a wall for an establishing high angle with my camera. Like a true newsreel man, I missed the beginning of the fight: the crowd, docile one moment, is struggling furiously the next. I leaped from the wall, the camera still running, and raced into the fight. People barged into me and knocked against the camera, blows were struck which registered as a jarring movement on the film. The clockwork motor ran out and I thought this a good time to regroup. 'Cut!' I yelled. No one took any notice. Some youths continued to kick a policeman they had pulled to the ground.

'All right, STOP!' I screamed. The fight carried on. So I carried on shooting.

The session was a great success. Thanks to Prince Marshall, publisher of *Old Motor* magazine and a new member of the unit, we spread eleven 1930 vehicles around the location. By accident we stumbled upon the secret of the atmosphere which had pervaded so many of our sessions. Extras were costumed correctly. Wherever they looked they saw vehicles of the correct period, posters, signboards. There was nothing, except the camera, to make them feel self-conscious—and that was out of sight much of the time.

Thanks to John Krish, another documentary company offered me a job. I surveyed my position at World Wide: it was a rewarding company to work for, but the freedom I needed to finish the film was gradually diminishing. I moved to Samaritan Films, and occupied a cutting room in the centre of Soho. In between Andrew's Woodfall assignments, we could now devote more time to *It Happened Here*.

131

Derek Hill, arranging a BBC programme called *Personal Cinema*, asked for an extract from our film. We chose the film-within-the-film, and were given ten days to produce a finished print. This deadline was the best thing that could have happened to us. We worked like fury. We shot all the outstanding scenes, assembled the results, wrote and recorded the commentary—again with Frank Phillips—and laid music and effects. Instead of cutting the negative, we made a dupe from the cutting copy, preserving all the scratches and abrasions, and heightening the effect of archive footage. We even got a review, from the editor of Punch (20 December 1961): '...a vastly ambitious piece... extraordinarily well done on shoestring resources... one sees the Reichswehr in apparently endless columns parading through Trafalgar Square and Whitehall...'

The *Jewish Chronicle*, however, was scandalised by our film. 'It was like viewing a Mosley meeting.' Were they blind to the irony? Judging by the telephone calls received by the BBC, several others shared this blindness. One man accused it of being nothing short of Nazi propaganda.

(Right) — *German troops enter St. Paul's Cathedral*

(Overleaf) — *The Parliament Square session*

14: False Alarm

January 1962. The start of another year increased our anxiety at lack of finance. Hearing Wardour Street rumours that a film was planned on the Forester account of the Invasion of England, we considered copyrighting the theme and title, and forming ourselves into a limited company. But one cannot make amateur films as a limited company.

Andrew and I were now holding regular meetings to discuss story and future plans. At one of these, I put forward the idea of taking off a month in June, five months ahead, in order to finish the main bulk of the picture. 'By that time, we would have a complete script, and we could persuade the most essential actors to take their holidays then. And by June we might have found some money.' Andrew agreed, but he pointed out that *Tom Jones* was due to begin in June, and he was signed to work on it. I was growing fatalistic about such setbacks. We turned our attention to the story, agreeing that big, spectacular scenes such as the invasion required a disproportionate amount of time and money and would have to be jettisoned. We should concentrate on the narrative.

Remembering the John Krish method of script-writing, I called on outside help. Jonathan Ingrams, one of our assistant directors, helped me to thrash out an outline for the rest of the picture. A colleague from Samaritan, Dinah Brooke, was the next to become involved. With the help of Andrew Sinclair, the novelist, she arranged a show for a producer, Theodora Olembert.

Madame Olembert shared their enthusiasm, and offered to distribute the picture through her company, Triangle Films. She had no immediate finance, but she was confident of obtaining it through close contacts. Realising that deliverance was at hand, Jonathan and I battered along our stubborn story-line. Andrew acted as a sort of piano-tuner, who could tell us when we struck a wrong note. One crashingly discordant section in his view was our favourite sequence—the Lidlington Project. This was an experimental medical centre where Pauline goes to work as a nurse. Andrew admitted that such places existed, but felt that our approach was too melodramatic. Concentration camp scenes were becoming a film cliché, and our idea about a terrifying medical research centre seemed to him unrealistic in the context of a scrupulously realistic film. We knew that a scene of this sort was a vital crux for the story, and we found his stubbornness frustrating.

2 April 1962: panic stations. Dinah Brooke informed us that Madame Olembert wanted a complete treatment by the following day; finance was in the offing. Since Jonathan was on location with his own film, I called upon Dinah's help. We completed the treatment in a day and a half, and despite Andrew's objections to Lidlington, we agreed to present a united front.

So far so good: Madame Olembert appeared to like the treatment. Now for the script. As far as the shooting script was concerned, it was essential that I wrote it on my own. Before describing a scene, I ran it through in my head, and this was an operation no one could help me with. Instead of dividing the treatment into scenes, as is customary, I broke it down into set-ups. This method enabled us to judge more accurately how many scenes to fit into a day's shooting. Occasionally, I had a query, and would telephone Andrew: 'Do you think we can get a barrage balloon?'

'I don't know. Write it in and we'll try.'

When each section was finished, I passed it to Andrew. He checked it carefully, altering some parts, adding others. The expected hiatus was struck a few days later, when Andrew made his last stand against my Lidlington idea. Removing this would mean completely re-thinking the last third of the film. This I refused to do.

'If you don't like an idea, don't kill it,' I said. 'Replace it with a better one.'

So Andrew went away and wrote a new version. 17 May 1962; I wrote in my diary: 'Mollo hates Brownlow script. Brownlow hates Mollo script. Where do we go from here?'

Madame Olembert had given us a fortnight to complete our script. Confident that we would soon be in production, Andrew had left Woodfall. It was therefore vital that the deadlock was broken. I suggested further research; if Andrew could find facts and figures about these experimental medical centres, I hoped he would be convinced. At the Wiener Library, he found a book called *The Hadamar Trial*. It was a horrifying, though moving, account of a Euthanasia Centre, a small German hospital for the mentally sick, which, having disposed of its patients, killed off regular consignments of Russian and Polish workers. These workers were treated with every kindness; they were given clean sheets, and matron gave cuddly toys to their children. During the night they were inoculated, ostensibly for infectious diseases, but the dose was lethal. Their bodies were buried in the kitchen garden. The element of tragedy was offset by irony and a degree of compassion—exactly what we wanted.

But Madame Olembert hated the script. Not because of the Lidlington scene, but because of our treatment of the Resistance Movement, something we had included virtually without argument. Furthermore, the National Film Finance Corporation, who saw the newsreel scene at Madame Olembert's behest, turned the film down flat.

Andrew visited Woodfall's office one afternoon, to pick up some papers. He encountered Tony Richardson.

'How's the film coming on?' he asked.

'Not very well,' replied Andrew.

'What happened?'

'The finance has fallen through.'

'Have you anything to show me?' asked Richardson.

We arranged a show for the following day. Both Tony

Richardson and Oscar Lewenstein liked what they saw. 'If you can prove the 16 mm material can be blown up,' said Richardson, 'we will consider financing you.'

Not quite able to believe what had happened to us, we chose a cross-section of our shooting, and put the negative into Humphries. Their optical department produced a 35 mm blow-up which Tony Richardson considered was good enough.

'If you can do the film for £3,000,' he said. 'We will find the money.'

15: The Rest Should Be Easy

At last our greatest ambition was realised—to make *It Happened Here* on 35 mm, with a professional company behind us. Woodfall made it clear, however, that no salaries would be paid, and the film would still have to be made in our spare time. They would not be involved in any way. They gave our company the name of Long Distance Films Ltd, which we thought sounded like a telegraph company. But it worked wonders with laboratories:

'Who's speaking?'

'Long Distance.'

'Oh! I'll put you through at once!'

Up to now we had spent every penny ourselves, so keeping within a tight budget presented no new problems. Having decided on what we needed, we worked out what we could afford, and boiled our lists down to bare essentials. Unlike professionals, we didn't have to cover ourselves. We could make decisions independently with complete confidence; this ability saved a great deal of money. On professional films, assistants are often terrified of incurring the director's displeasure. Asked to select one costume, they choose ten, just in case the director dislikes their first choice.

People have often asked how it was possible to make the film with two directors. Creative partnerships, particularly successful ones, are rare enough to arouse instant suspicion: who is the sleeping partner? *It Happened Here* became so much a part of our lives that the borderline between our activities was blurred. At one time or another, we did everything on the picture bar the actual processing. As far as production went, we worked as a team most obviously on the big action sequences. Dialogue scenes cannot be directed by two people without thoroughly confusing the actors, and these were my responsibility. Andrew set these scenes up, kept production running smoothly and was always available for advice.

We made no concessions to the fact that everyone was working for nothing. When someone came on a session, we expected him to give his heart and soul to the picture, regardless of personal comfort. *It Happened Here* was a labour of love, made by people who liked each other, and who understood each other. It was carried to completion by enthusiasm.

How we got through our first sync session, however, is still a mystery. They were two of the toughest days we had so far experienced. We tried to shoot the suburban interior, in which Pauline meets Honor, and Honor tries to persuade her to join the Immediate Action Organisation (the collaborationist group). I had relinquished my position as cameraman; since I found it hard to judge performances through a viewfinder. Jonathan Ingrams took over. We borrowed an Auricon camera, a machine with which we were both unfamiliar.

Shooting began ominously. Honor felt extremely unwell; in fact, she was sick at regular, fifteen minute intervals. Each time we were ready to shoot, poor Honor would have to dash from the room. Then the sound recordist, down the corridor, reported he could hear camera noise. The motor echoed in that tiny room. We buried Jonathan underneath an eiderdown; it was already stiflingly hot because of the lights. The window had to be locked shut to keep out the noise of traffic. Jonathan nearly suffocated, but the eiderdown absorbed most of the camera noise. The camera changed its tune to a high-pitched scraping sound, which we correctly divined as magazine scrape. The roll of film had formed a ridge, and this was scraping against the inside of the magazine. Squeeeak, squeeeak, squeeeak. Jonathan smoothed out the roll inside a changing bag. Ready once again—and the camera jammed. When the film was re-threaded, the switch failed. Then the sync-pulse plug developed a fault. Disaster piled upon disaster so fast that we began to find the situation funny. We found that the zoom lens wobbled, and was unreliable. The Miller Fluid Head was too stiff for sharp movements. We had microphone breakdowns, we had cable breakdowns. We found that tape two was six DBs above tape one; this meant that the volume of one would not match the volume of the others. And to crown it all, just as we were making some headway, the sound recordist went home. He was a professional, hired at slightly below the union minimum. And you cannot argue with professionals.

Sunday, as far as disasters go, went as stupefyingly as Saturday. Whenever we tried to shoot, the world of suburbia conspired to stop us. We were on a direct flight path for London Airport. We also had the gentler, but equally irritating noise of lawnmowers. Motor-bikes revved up, children screamed, babies cried, cats yowled. And from the distance came the sound of a Salvation Army band.

Too much in despair to cope with this new interruption, I sent Andrew to stop the noise. He came back with the news that the band refused to stop. We endured two more hymns, then sent Andrew out to try again in the name of Christian charity. The music ceased, and Andrew ran back. 'Quickly,' he shouted. 'Get the shot while they're praying!'

No catalogue of catastrophes can do more than hint at the real cause of tension: the wasted time. The players' performances are affected, the technicians become irritable, and the director is in an agony of suspense. With equipment on hire, a location available only for that one weekend, players who have come great distances, and a tight schedule to follow, the suspense affects the stomach like the last reel of a Hitchcock picture.

The rushes of this painful session were the final disaster. They were not merely disappointing. They were devoid of picture. There was nothing, beyond vague shadows, to indicate all the work we had done. We attacked the laboratories; they denied responsibility. There was nothing wrong with the camera mechanism, beyond the failures we had already experienced.

Jonathan had been meticulous with both focus and exposure. How strange that a simple scene with two people in one room should have caused so much trouble!

The following day, I read of a unit who had had a slightly worse experience than ours. An Indian crew shooting in the forests during the rains had been struck by a thunderbolt. The cameraman had been killed...

16: Detained in Hospital

The riot scene was a highly complex action sequence, but it was a rest cure after our last experience. Our main prop was a 1929 Reo coach, which Andrew and I had helped Prince Marshall restore; now painted field-grey it served as a riot bus, with the lightning-flash insignia of the Immediate Action Organisation on the side. The bus held thirty-six Blackshirts. Early on the morning of the session, it passed the headquarters of the British National-Socialist Movement. Three members, one in breeches and jackboots, stood chatting on the pavement. Suddenly, they spotted the riot bus, and stared as though at an apparition. As soon as they had recovered from their surprise, they leaped on motor-cycles and gave chase. But the bus doubled back into a parallel street and threw them off.

Our location was uncomfortably close to the Nazi headquarters, but they never located it, even when the bus roared through Holland Park with its bell clanging. Local residents, however, decided that the worst had happened and telephoned the Special Branch: 'Colin Jordan has mobilised!'

We had already shot one street fight, for the propaganda film, and I was anxious for a different style. I wanted this riot to be shot with swift, smooth tracking shots, which would hurtle the audience right into the fight. That chasm which separates ideas from reality brought about my downfall. Smooth tracking shots require special equipment. We had only an ancient wooden dolly mounted on rails. The rails were not long enough to provide the effect I was after, and I had to resort to a hand- held camera. However, sharp intercutting between the fight, and shots of Pauline clinging like Pearl White to the riot bus, give this scene a distinctive flavour.

We were making faster progress, despite the suburb setback, than at any time since the picture began. Nevertheless, because

143

An officer from the Immediate Action Organisation takes Pauline to a pub for lunch, and becomes involved in a brawl

144

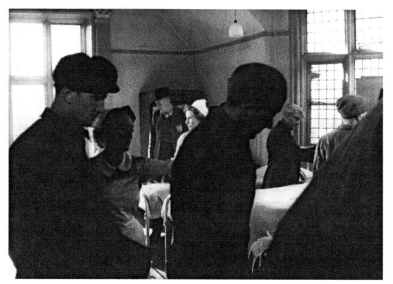

Russian and Polish workers, suffering from TB,
arrive in the sunlit hospital ward

of our professional commitments, progress was not fast enough. We decided to tackle a lengthy dialogue sequence: the controversial Lidlington scene. The script described Lidlington as 'a large Edwardian country house, set in its own beautiful, well-kept grounds.' Finding this location was difficult; eventually our enquiries led to the mock-Gothic residence of W. S. Gilbert, of Gilbert and Sullivan. Named Grim's Dyke, it was a specialist hospital for the rehabilitation of TB patients, exactly as described in the script.

Now that we were progressing to 35 mm, we needed a cameraman familiar with 35 mm. I recalled a camera assistant from World Wide who had done one day's work on the picture: Peter Suschitzky. I asked him round to discuss the matter. He brought some photographs he had taken in Brazil. They were brilliant. He was clearly a talented stills photographer, and he knew how an Arriflex worked. I decided to take a gamble and sign him up as our cameraman.

145

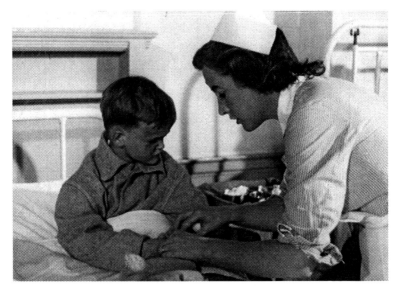

Pauline inoculates a Polish boy

I knew Suschitzky would be familiar with most aspects of camerawork, but I was not satisfied that he could light interiors. A most important element of the Lidlington sequence was to be its quality of light. As Pauline entered the hallway, it had to be gloomy and ominous; as she joined the other nurses for tea, the room had to be sunlit and welcoming. Could Suschitzky achieve this at his first attempt? We could not afford a second.

The first shot we made on 35 mm was the long shot of the tea-table at Lidlington, when Pauline enters to be greeted by the doctor: 'Ah, we've been expecting you. I'm in charge here.' The doctor then introduces the rest of the staff.

Peter had done miracles with the lighting, and sunshine flooded through the windows despite the fact that it was raining outside. I stopped worrying about the photography; now it was the performances that bothered me. We had to shoot Lidlington in one concentrated week. Non-professionals were seldom available during working hours so, for the first time, we resorted to professional actors. One of these professionals, at the cost of £10 a day, was fulfilling my worst fears:

'My name is — —,' the actor hesitated.

'Cut!' That's thirty bob gone already, I thought.

'All right, let's try it again. Turn over sound.'

'Running.'

'Camera.'

'Running.'

'Mark it!'

Johanna Roeber, our new continuity girl, announced the number and banged the clapper-board. There was a momentary silence. I took a deep breath.

'Action!'

'My name is… er… ' It was too late to find a replacement. We had to limp through sentence by sentence.

At the Lidlington session, the unit consisted of five people: Peter Suschitzky on camera, Johanna Roeber, continuity, Andrew, myself and a sound recordist. This pattern continued for the rest of the film, although extra production assistants were recruited for complicated exteriors. (The average professional feature unit numbers about twenty-five.)

Peter Suschitzky, immaculately dressed under all conditions, greeted catastrophes with a bland stare and never grew ruffled or angry. Since he had no assistant, he had to light the set, load the magazines, operate the camera and follow focus all by himself. At this time, he was 22 years old.

I doubt whether we would have survived the gruelling week at Lidlington without Johanna Roeber. She supported our morale under the worst of circumstances: even when Peter and I had been concussed by two-kilowatt lamps, falling from a considerable height, she somehow kept us going. (This was the first session on which she had worked with Peter Suschitzky; she later married him.)

Pauline displayed the greatest heroism; she was frequently struck by severe migraine, yet none of us knew this until the fi-

Pauline leaves Lidlington under close arrest

lm was over. Again and again she had to act as a foil for other players, having her own close-ups done very quickly very late at night

Because our unit was so small she also helped in dozens of other ways, some of which would have caused Equity members to walk out on strike.

Despite the grimness of the sequence, the comedy continued. When Pauline, wandering through the grounds, comes across the graves in the kitchen garden, her expression of horror was secured just before she burst into laughter. 'What's the matter?' I asked, crossly. She pointed behind the camera. Andrew was hanging upside down from a branch, like a monkey, scattering autumn leaves over the graves...

Bart Allison, a fine professional actor who played the old caretaker of the hospital, could not drive. But a scene in the script called for him to drive Pauline from the local station. 'Don't worry,' we assured him, 'we'll teach you.'

The first lesson took place in a field near a main road. Bart was shown the basic elements of driving, and told to manoeuvre his vehicle, an elderly Bentley, out of the field and on to the road. Andrew held up traffic.

'What's going on?' a motorist asked Andrew.

'We're making a film,' he answered.

'What's it about?'

'The German occupation of England.'

Suddenly, the Bentley shot out of the field, zig-zagged wildly on the road and crashed into a telegraph pole.

'Looks very exciting!' said the motorist, and drove up for a closer look.

Greatly relieved by the successful conclusion of this sequence, we began to set up for the next blockbuster, the Fletcher sequence.

A vital role still had to be filled: that of Dr Fletcher, the anti-Fascist who hides the wounded partisan. This character had taken shape in my mind as a combination of Dick Jobson and a producer friend at World Wide. Neither of them could take part, so we turned to Spotlight, the actors' directory. The directory fell open at a picture of Sebastian Shaw.

'Now that's the sort of person we want,' I said. 'Not that we could ever get him!'

'Why not?' asked Andrew.

'Why not!' We telephoned his agent, and arranged a meeting that same night—at 11.30 p.m. Sebastian Shaw, a star of the British cinema in the thirties and forties, who had since achieved prominence on the stage, *was* ideal. He said he would play the role only if he liked the script. He read it, and agreed to do the part for a nominal fee. But he stipulated two conditions: if the film were shown commercially, he would be paid his fee, and he would have complete freedom to re-write his dialogue.

We agreed to both conditions.

For some unaccountable reason, Peter Suschitzky lost confidence at the beginning of this sequence. I told him that the basement location—a real basement—had to be lit in two distinct moods. The first had to be bright and sunny, the second, sombre and dismal. For the bright and sunny scene, which he had handled so well at Lidlington, he called in his father, cameraman Wolfgang Suschitzky. Depending on someone else, when you lack confidence in the first place, is a fatal mistake. When Wolfgang had departed, Peter had no one to lean on.

'What about those double shadows?' I asked, pointing to some candlesticks. They were casting not double, but quintuple shadows—a physical impossibility in a room with one source of light.

'They'll be all right. You won't notice them.'

When a cameraman tells you that, don't believe him. Anything you can see with the naked eye will be picked up by the camera. Next morning, when we saw rushes, the interior of our basement looked like the set for a Merton Park commercial. I was beyond consolation.

The following day's rushes showed a tremendous improvement in lighting and atmosphere. Peter had quickly grasped the essentials of this kind of shooting and now he endeavoured to preserve the atmosphere rather than light it out of existence.

Not being able to afford a cutting-room assistant, even on a part-time basis, I synched-up, logged and broke down my own rushes. This was not the chore I had anticipated, for it familiarised me with the material, and I found a close examination of my mistakes very instructive. This careful inspection also brought to light the true quality of Pauline's performance. She and Sebastian Shaw played well together, so I was astonished to receive a letter from Pauline, written in the train as she returned to New Radnor: 'Now I know how you can be depressed with rushes. Never again. Fiona Leland' (who played Fletcher's wife, Helen) 'and Sebastian seemed alive, real people, and I look like a vicious moron walking up and down Belsize Square. I shall be livid if I let you down on this film. If we had

The arrest of the Fletchers, Sebastian Shaw with pipe, Fiona Leland as Mrs. Fletcher. The lower picture is a frame-enlargement from an out-take. The scene was shot in mid-and close- shots, but an extreme long-shot proved more effective.

*Pauline, with Jenny Holt, at the passing-out parade of the
Immediate Action Organisation*

not got so far, I'd say get someone else, but I honestly feel that
the lack of expression on my face is disastrous and will ruin the
whole thing for you. I felt awful all day thinking of the final
result.'

We had many anxieties on this picture, but Pauline was certainly not one of them. Her underplaying—her 'lack of expression'—was essential, for the entire film was in this key.

17: The Nazis Speak

We decided to cast Frank Bennett, whose party we had attended back in 1960, in a prominent role as an English Fascist officer. He knew we were presenting the Nazi case accurately and objectively, and he therefore accepted. Our aim was to allow the Nazis to discuss their beliefs, to bring their sickness into the open, and to condemn themselves out of their own mouths. We hoped to show that Fascism meant not only concentration camps and brutality; we wanted to bring it closer to the conscience of the audience, some of whom might agree with the Nazis without suspecting that their opinions were shared by extremists.

We set up for the discussion scene in the lounge of the Rembrandt Hotel; its decor, unchanged since the 1930s, provided an ideal backdrop. We gathered the group together—among them were two Nazis and one Fascist—gave them drinks, and let them mellow before we took our first shot. In the story, they have just returned from the propaganda film. As we come upon them, Pauline is listening to Frank Bennett, describing the early days with Mosley. Then she refers directly to the film-within-a-film—to the scene which showed blitzed London, while the narrator talked of 'these fruits of Jewish control'.

'Why did the film blame the Jews for the Blitz?' she asks. We set the camera on the Nazis and fired questions like this, as at a live television discussion. Some questions were too awkward, and Bennett held his hand in front of the lens. But all the replies used in the sequence were spontaneous. For instance:

THOMAS: It's not that the Aryans are so superior—but every race is superior to the Jew. The Jew has no home. The Jew is a parasite race. The Jew waits for a civilisation to be established, and establishes himself on it. A flea on a dog.

BENNETT: Yes, fleas can live on a dog, but fleas can't live

on fleas. Send them all to Madagascar, that's the simplest way.

THOMAS (off): ...and let them cheat one another instead of cheating the people they've lived off for the past centuries.

Apart from the anti-Semitic diatribe, the Nazis brought up the subject of euthanasia, and the discussion sequence became a vital precursor to Lidlington.

The Fascist said, simply: 'Euthanasia? It's a surgical operation, getting rid of useless matter, useless tissue. Any doctor does it ten times a day, if it's necessary.'

Pauline asked: 'If you had a small child who contracted some disease that left him paralysed, as well he might, would he then be just waste tissue to be got rid of?'

'Exactly,' said the Fascist.

'Certainly,' said Bennett.

The completion of the discussion scene was a great boost to our morale. Even if the rest of the picture failed, we could depend on one scene of real value. No film since the end of the war had given National-Socialists *carte blanche* to express their opinions, with the result that few people had a clear idea of what they stood for, or of the insidious threat they represented. But it wasn't long before we, too, were denied the right to free speech over this sequence...

The film we were now making had little in common with the film we were making in Berwick St John. As our attitudes had changed, so the film had altered stylistically. No longer was there the slightest hint of the conventional war film. The military sequences, intended to recur throughout the picture, were now relegated to beginning and end. The psychological effects of occupation interested us now as much as the atmosphere. Sensational scenes were deleted or carefully underscored. Had the film been made within the first year or so, it might well have been a lurid action picture. Now we had learned the value of understatement, the effectiveness of restraint. Andrew and I had always visualised the picture in a different way. My wild ideas of invasion and atom bombings had always been sobered by Andrew's practical view of reality. Now our approaches were coinciding. We understood each other better, our ideas grew from a common ground and we worked together more efficiently.

The film had changed in other directions, too; working on a semi-professional basis, with equipment on hire, meant that spending time no longer saved us money. In the old days, we could afford to wait for a day or a week to secure some vital prop at half price. Now we were paying for the hire of the camera, ancillary equipment, tape recorder, tracking equipment and sometimes even vehicles.

To stay within our budget, Andrew scheduled the script ruthlessly, and I found it hard to work fast *and* achieve results which satisfied us both. Occasionally, a player would reveal unexpected talent and we could race ahead of schedule. One such player was Miles Halliwell, who appeared as an IA lecturer. Having been coached by Frank Bennett on the tenets of Nazism, Halliwell brilliantly improvised his lecture, delivering it so well it sounded as though he believed it, which was very far from the truth. Thanks to his effortless performance, I was able to elaborate a static mid-shot into an intricate tracking shot. The camera followed Halliwell slowly from side to side as he paced the room, gradually coming closer until the whole lecture ended in a close-up. To be able to bring some cinematic value to a dialogue scene was a great relief, but performances of this calibre were all too rare.

The big funeral sequence was staged in the Albany Street Territorial Army drill hall. The complete dressing for this sequence—uniforms, flags, drapes, even the huge silver sword dominating one wall—was made by Andrew, and the entire Mollo family was press-ganged into sewing brassards and buttons on to tunics. A firm of funeral directors supplied a coffin, wreaths and a set of candlesticks last used at King George VI's lying-in-state. The coffin was draped with Fascist flags; behind it was a rostrum, flanked by standards from each country

155

within the British Isles.Now Peter Suschitzky was faced for the first time with elaborate effect lighting. Alarmed at the prospect, he once again suggested calling upon the assistance of his father. I told him I would like his father to light the film, but we couldn't have two cameramen. 'We are willing to take the risk. You must, too.'

With nightfall, the lighting was complete, and the atmosphere impressively Wagnerian. It was too real for one man: he took a swift look inside the drill hall, took off his uniform and fled. We handed out song sheets and rehearsed the *Horst Wessel* in English. The effect was cacophonous; as someone put it:'This sounds more like a Hoarse Festival'.*

The funeral took only five hours to shoot. The unit and many of the extras squeezed into the theatre at Humphries to see the rushes. They exceeded our wildest hopes. Peter had done a magnificent job of lighting.

With our confidence soaring, we did two days on the training montages. On the interior, we did fifty-four set-ups in a normal working day. On the exterior, sixty-seven. We began to wonder why the picture had taken so long. At last we were within sight of the end.

*In July, 1967, we were informed by the Mechanical Copyright Society that the *Horst Wessel Lied* was still protected by copyright. 'But Horst Wessel was shot in a prostitute's bedroom by a Communist!' I protested. 'Who took up the copyright—the Communist?' Evidently it was a respected German music publisher, to whom we were forced to pay £360 for 2½ minutes.

Peter Suschitzky lines up a tracking shot for the passing out parade

Miles Haliwell, with Colonel Percy Binns

18: Final Surrender

Because of lack of time, and the risk of refusal, we did not obtain police permission for a short session held in the Harrow Road area. We set up for a scene showing the aftermath of a massacre. Peter Suschitzky complained that somebody's feet were in shot. A group of youths had gathered to watch, and they were standing too near to the camera.

'Would you mind moving back?' asked Andrew. The boys refused. 'Go on, please. Move back. We're trying to film.' The boys stayed where they were, so I moved the set-up. The boys walked forward into the shot. Andrew, forgetting his own rule never to lay hands on bystanders, pushed one of the boys. In a flash, the boy lowered his head and butted him in the face. Andrew crashed to the pavement. For a moment everybody froze. Then Andrew climbed to his feet and struck the boy on the nose. The boy shot back, startled. Blood trickled from his nose. He whipped off his belt, on to which had been stitched a bicycle chain, and began whirling it round his head. I stepped between them, feeling that Andrew had successfully proved the point of the film—that one should never meet violence with violence. 'Get out of the way,' said the boy, 'I'm goin' to get 'im.' We told him to go home and stop being a bloody nuisance.

The boy vanished, but we knew the danger had not passed. We hurriedly packed up the camera gear, and, like western pioneers, pushed the women into our ambulance and sent Chris Slaughter and Peter to summon reinforcements from the police station. Then we waited. No sign of the police. We were alone and vulnerable when fifteen youths advanced along the street like western gunfighters. They had clearly come to defend their injured comrade.

But as soon as they realised we were not a rival gang, and were simply trying to work, they moved off.

The younger boys, however, remained, and the original troublemaker had another go at Andrew. 'Look out, he's got a chopper,' yelled Dorothy Hodgetts, our ambulance driver. The boy leaped at Andrew, pulling the hood of his anorak over his head. We were just in time to prevent him bringing a milk crate down on Andrew's head. Several others were now involved, and Christopher Slaughter returned at the right psychological moment. He was wearing police uniform. It was the wartime uniform, but it was enough to alarm our assailants.

'The police won't come,' said Slaughter. 'They say it's the wrong division.'

As if to give the lie to his words, a police car drew up, and a superintendent emerged. He looked at the motley gang and remarked, 'Just as I thought. Wrong division.' He climbed back into his car and drove off. We felt bitterly resentful, like pioneers besieged by Indians who watch the cavalry stop, survey the scene, mutter 'wrong state' and gallop away.

The arrival of the real police, however, had lent authenticity to the actor. The boys slowly circled us, aware that Slaughter was probably not real, but unwilling to take the chance. At long last another police car drove up, and the gang dispersed. Dorothy rushed up and cried, 'One of them had a chopper!'

'Yes, madam,' said the policeman, wearily. 'They've all got choppers.'

During these sessions, we kept up our attendances at the National Film Theatre. At a show of von Stroheim's *Merry Widow*, we met Stanley Kubrick, whose *Paths of Glory* had set a new standard for historical reconstruction. Kubrick had begun his career making pictures on his own.

'My biggest problem was raw stock,' he said. 'How are you doing for 35 mm film?'

'Pretty badly,' we admitted.

The derelict street off the Harrow Road where the fight broke out

'Well, here's what you do,' he said. 'Call my secretary, and I'll arrange for you to have the short ends from *Dr Strangelove.*'

We used Stanley Kubrick's stock on the big surrender scene, the climax of our years of location shooting. Preparations began on an optimistic note, when a Territorial battalion offered us fifty men—a fully independent unit, with bivouacs and vehicles. We laid on a coach to transport our other extras to the location, the little village of Eashing in Surrey, and hired a barn from a farmer to accommodate them overnight. Since we had been guaranteed the TA unit, we asked only fifty of our extras. But the TA unit never arrived. Then the farmer withdrew permission for his barn; he had noticed our extras smoking, and could see his barn bursting into flames. It was 7.30 in the evening, pouring with rain in a lonely Surrey village; we had nowhere to sleep and not enough extras for the following day.

While Andrew looked for somewhere to spend the night, I tried hard to think of a source of extras. Earlier in the day, I had heard of an approved school in the neighbourhood. Assistant director Graham Samuel drove me to the school. It was a converted house; Borstal boys played table-tennis before an Adam fireplace.

The headmaster was surprisingly friendly and seemed to think a day's filming was just what his boys needed. He offered to bring fifty seventeen and eighteen year olds the following day.

When we got back to the village, we found cast and unit billeted in the meeting room of the local pub. In the bar, Frank Bennett was celebrating Hitler's birthday. One man, who had bought him a pint, announced that he was Jewish. Bennett emptied the beer on the floor. 'I will not accept your drink, but I will buy you one. What will you have?'

'A double Scotch,' said the Jew.

That night, Frank Bennett met with a mysterious accident. Dead drunk, he arrived at our billet, the side of his face covered with blood. He explained later that he had tripped down some steps, but it was suspected that he had been beaten up. We needed a casualty, so next morning we put him in SS uniform. Bennett may have been perverse, but he never lost his sense of humour. 'I know how you can finish the film,' he said. 'Pauline can prostrate herself with grief over my body, and you can end with a close-up of her tears falling on my face.'

Working with walkie-talkies, we shot the main surrender, two detachments of SS troops emerging from the village, their hands on their helmets. The first group, ordered and precise, consisted of our own extras. The second, shambling and cowed by defeat, were the Borstal boys. One of the two officers leading the surrender was a former officer in the SS, who had surrendered in 1945 in this same fashion to the Americans. He said later that the staging of the scene was so real it had been a traumatic experience for him.

The massacre of the English collaborationist troops is shown to be the act of extremists. At its height, a jeepload of American soldiers arrives. We cut away to the shooting. When we cut back to the jeep, an American is standing on the bonnet, taking photographs. Anxious to be as subtle as possible, I chose a set-up too far away from the jeep, and destroyed the irony of the scene. Audiences think the American is simply gazing at the massacre through binoculars; they cannot always spot his Leica.

The rushes of the surrender sequence dissatisfied me, for no reason I could put my finger on. Andrew and the others were not over-excited, either. This reaction was an anti-climax after the riotous reception for the funeral scene. But film is an unpredictable medium. Sometimes rushes look better than the cut sequence. At other times, they only come to life when cut together. As it happened, the funeral gave us editing headaches; the surrender cut together easily. But the session had been costly: the Borstal boys had ripped and razored the badges off every uniform.

Following pages — *The surrender scene*

165

19: Picking Up the Pieces

The truth of the old adage that directors should not edit their own films was proved to me during these preliminary stages. Again and again, I included shots that should have been discarded, merely because they had taken hours to accomplish. Sometimes I neglected to include enough establishing material, because I knew the geography of each location so well. Gradually, I managed to cast off my directorial possessiveness, and the clinical instincts of an editor took over.

Because Tony Richardson planned to leave for New York, we were asked to have a rough-cut ready very swiftly. The day before the show we still had four sequences to cut. Andrew brought up camp beds, blankets and coffee and we worked through the night. At 2.00 a.m. I collapsed on the bed, the surrender scene still incomplete. I could do no more; it had defeated me. I lay for a few minutes, trying to sleep. Suddenly, I thought of a solution, leaped out of bed, and carried on working until the next problem arose; then a quick think on the bed, and back to work. It was an ideal arrangement.

Tony Richardson's overall enthusiasm for the picture compensated for the penetrating criticisms he made. But he went abroad, and although Oscar Lewenstein liked the film very much, we gathered that none of the other Woodfall people were as enthusiastic. Our contact, Mike Holden, told us frankly that he didn't think we would get any more money.

We mounted a series of screenings for potential distributors. Kenneth Shipman, of the Shipman and King circuit, was the first: 'A most unpleasant film,' he said. 'I want nothing to do with it.' A full-scale screening was arranged for sixteen high-powered film industry figures. Two turned up: James Woolf and Paul Fletcher, of the National Film Finance Corporation. James Woolf got up at the end of the picture, and walked out without a word. Paul Fletcher was more encouraging, but he regretted that the NFFC could not help us to finish the picture, or to get it distributed.

We began the old, depressing search for finance, and with the limited money left in the budget, pressed on with the negative cutting of the 16 mm section. The job took much longer than necessary, mainly because of the large amount of uncatalogued material. We had a fright when the neg-cutting people told us that twenty-one separate sections were missing. I began an all-out search; there was nothing at home, nothing at Andrew's home, only one can in the cutting room. The others were with the neg-cutting people. They hadn't checked carefully enough. On top of this, their bill came to more than three times their estimated price. We refused to pay more than the agreed figure, so they threatened legal action.

Meanwhile, our screenings to distributors were costing a great deal of money and getting us nowhere. At a showing to British Lion, Frank Launder walked out in the middle. The Boulting Brothers stayed on, but we gathered that neither of them liked the picture. Charles Cooper, of Contemporary Films, considered the film anti-Semitic, a reaction which flabbergasted us. Producer Daniel Angel stormed out of a screening after a mere forty minutes, telephoned Woodfall and berated Oscar Lewenstein for allowing 'this Nazi picture' to be made. The film even upset some of our most generous supporters. 'We would never have collaborated like that,' said one. 'We would have fought the Germans in the streets with broomsticks. The British could never surrender.'

February 1964: we were approached by a consortium of sound editors from Pinewood. They offered to take the picture over, to lay tracks and to dub it. The cost? £5,000. We thanked them very much, but explained that the whole picture had cost little more than that. Instead, we secured the services of George Fisher, sound editor on *Seance on a Wet Afternoon*. He generously agreed to work for next to nothing, and Woodfall at last

A German band marches through Chester Terrace,
Regent's Park

consented to see the film through the dubbing stages.

A contact in a sound studio agreed to stay after work for a post-sync sound session. He persuaded his crew to do the same, and they worked for half-price. We hired the best-known effects expert, a miracle worker called Beryl Mortimer. A wizard with footsteps, she could supply many other incidental effects. Recently, she had padded on all fours in a box of sand, recording the hoof-beats of camels for *Lawrence of Arabia*. The sound studio laid various surfaces on the floor—a couple of paving stones and a short length of gravel. Beryl Mortimer and her assistant, equipped with footwear ranging from army boots to bedroom slippers, watched the picture loop once, then recorded the effects in perfect sync. If Pauline was shown crossing a road, mounting a pavement and running up some steps, Beryl supplied the noises with uncanny precision: the little hes-

171

Soldiers appraise girls on the Embankment, London

itations on the edge of the pavement, the flatter sound on the steps—these simple noises brought each shot alive. When several characters appeared at once, the loop was run twice, and Beryl and her assistant became a crowd. They raced through 31 loops in a little over two hours.

To post-synchronise the dialogue, we needed several New Radnor villagers. We hadn't reckoned with the cost of bringing them to London, so I decided to take a portable recorder to New Radnor and record the lines wild. Theoretically, this was a ridiculous idea. How could these lines ever match those spoken years before for a silent camera? In practice, however, the system worked very well. I recorded three or four versions of the same line, at varying speeds of delivery. The words had been transcribed at the time of shooting, and although it took hours of patient work at a moviola, I managed to make all the lines fit. The system was flawed only by my use of a tape-recorder with a fixed speed of 1⅞ i.p.s. Had I recorded at 7½ i.p.s., there would have been no problem. But 1⅞ i.p.s. is not a professional speed, and to transfer it to 35 mm magnetic, our sound people were forced to adapt their equipment. My original recording was adequate, but their transfer was muffled. Since the quality of sound cannot be judged from a moviola, the truth hit us when it was too late to re-record. The opening dialogue sequence is therefore somewhat indistinct.

These post-shooting stages—editing, track-laying, dubbing, neg-cutting and so on—were as full of pitfalls as the actual shooting. But the problems, being more technical, were less colourful.

During shooting we were assisted by enthusiasts. During the post-production stages, we moved into a realm occupied solely by professionals. You may have found amateur cameramen and amateur sound recordists, but you would never have found amateur dubbing mixers or laboratory technicians. This was an area in which one either submitted to fixed prices, or tried to coax reductions from hard-headed businessmen who had nothing whatever to gain from your custom. However much you wooed professionals, you could not offer them what they most desired—prestige. You could not compete with MGM or Rank, and anything less received proportionately less attention.

Our sound editor laid his tracks sensitively and intelligently. We hired a dubbing theatre reputed to be the best in the country, and a dubbing mixer who was skilful and resourceful. But his assistant was a sort of moon man; he stared at the controls as though he had never seen them before, and did his level best not to operate them. When forced to do so, he would fade in the noise of heavy traffic over a long shot of an empty field. How the dubbing mixer endured him was a constant wonder to us. Whenever he blundered, which was frequently, the mixer would sigh sadly, and start all over again. I admired his tolerance until I realised that we were financing it.

173

During the dubbing, the funeral sequence caused us great anxiety. Andrew had taken an intense dislike to it; he thought that it failed to create the right atmosphere. He was unhappy about his art direction, and about the way I had shot it. 'It should have been stark and simple, like Leni Riefenstahl,' he concluded. I was unhappy, too, though for different reasons. The tracks did not match each other, the recording was flat and undramatic and no amount of echo seemed to help. Reluctantly, I agreed to cut it out, but soon my decision began to bother me. The scene was necessary to the picture, and its removal suggested a display of bravado. We had already lost our battle scene, incorporating it in a montage, because it held up the progress of our story. Were we not removing another spectacular scene, just to prove we could do it?

'No,' said Andrew. 'The scene is fundamentally wrong.' He was adamant that it should not go back in the picture. I was determined that it should. So I spent the weekend completely recutting it. We viewed the result, and Andrew agreed that it had been greatly improved. This experience again illustrates the value of our partnership. Without the opposition, the scene would never have been recut. It would have remained in the film in its inferior form. Even so, it took a further two hours of dubbing time before this three-minute sequence finally worked.

26 May 1964: *It Happened Here* was finished. The realisation intoxicated us and we took our sound editor to lunch in the hope of becoming really intoxicated. 'This afternoon we take it easy,' I wrote in my diary. 'I think we both know there will never be quite this moment again.'

GREAT BRITAIN

SWEDEN

HUNGARY

NO ENTRY

LTD UPSIDE DOWN

FRANCE

20: Festival Time

The end of production heralded a whole new era of problems. The least expected was a request from an indispensable member of the unit for a percentage of the profits. We were dismayed that our comradeship should so suddenly change to a business agreement. How could profits be fairly divided between people who had worked on the film for years and spent all their money, and one who had worked for seven months and been paid his expenses? We asked him to leave the sharing out of the spoils to us; we had Pauline to think about, as well as professionals who had insisted on a participation. But no; we had to have an agreement in writing. Eventually, we settled on a participation arrangement—2½ per cent—with the result that he got nothing. But then, neither did we; so we were back to square one, and we could have avoided the bitterness. We didn't make the film for money, and he didn't help us for money.

The optical track, made from the magnetic master dub, was transferred by the dubbing assistant, and it was as skilful as one might expect. It sounded as though it had been recorded through an old sock. All the exciting effects we had heard on magnetic were smoothed to a flat monotone. Anguished, I took the track back. The dubbing mixer considered it perfect.

Ever since, criticism has been levelled against the sound. In theatres with below-standard equipment, the dialogue is frequently inaudible. Yet, with the exception of the opening sequence, the entire film was recorded by professionals; it was dubbed, transferred and printed by professionals. Later, a second optical track was made and there was a considerable impr-

Left — The London Film Festival display, at the Odeon, Haymarket1964

ovement. By that time, however, most of the prints had been made.

We hovered over every stage of the combined print, checking picture and sound tests, viewing the answer print, going over the grading alterations and testing the patience of Humphries, the long-suffering laboratory. The 16 mm sections gave us our greatest headache. One laboratory, Filmatic, produced the fine-grains. Another, Kays, produced first-class 35 mm blow-up negatives, but they accidentally ruined the fine-grains. Back we went to Filmatic, paying for the whole operation twice, because Kays, in common with all other laboratories, accept no liability for mishaps. Meanwhile, Filmatic had notched the 16 mm negative twice. When we came to make a 16 mm print, Humphries refused to proceed, explaining that the two sets of notches (controlling the printer lights) would throw their machines awry. They also complained that the negative joins (the responsibility of yet another firm) were falling apart.

Despite these headaches, we were delighted when the Federation of British Film Makers suggested that our film should go to the Venice Film Festival. We arranged a screening for the organiser, Signor Chiarini. Chiarini attacked the film on artistic grounds, which was novel, since everyone else had concentrated on its political implications. 'We have very high standards at Venice,' he said, 'very high standards. This is just not good enough. But don't let this discourage you boys.'

About the only thing that didn't discourage us at this stage was a show arranged by Richard Roud, of the British Film Institute, for Chris Marker and his producer, Wim van Leer. Roud was undecided about the film, but Marker raved. This enthusiasm from a fellow film-maker was the first glimmer of hope we had had for months. Wim van Leer, with unprecedented generosity, telephoned the next day and offered us financial assistance. He was in England for the presentation of his play *Patent Pending*, a brilliant study of the Final Solution, which had itself been attacked by certain Jews. Yet van Leer

178

lived in Israel, and had been involved in smuggling Jews from Nazi Germany. He warned us that we, too, would be subject to attack. 'But anything I can do to help,' he said, 'just let me know.'

With the loss of the Venice Festival, we accepted the next offer to come along—the Cork Festival. Since Cork was my father's home town, and since Pauline went to school nearby, it seemed appropriate.

The publicity put out by Cork attracted the notice of Peter Evans of the *Daily Express*. Could he see the picture? Certainly, we said, provided there were no reviews until the picture was released. He agreed. He saw the film with Leonard Mosley; and, a few days later, the *Express* ran a special review, with picture, to our mingled consternation and delight. We feared that other critics would resent precedence being given to one newspaper, but as it happened, the advance publicity did us a great deal of good.

'If you ever have a chance to see it,' wrote Leonard Mosley, 'you will be shattered.' He added that the picture had all the faults of a film made on a shoestring, but he did not catalogue these faults and the overall tone of the review was favourable.

The morning of its appearance, 24 August 1964, the telephone never stopped ringing: BBC, Granada, various distributors, even the Russian Sovexportfilm. The BBC put a brief plug on *Today* which produced an invitation from *Tonight*. The *Tonight* team, or at least the young assistants we met, had seen the film at a special screening, and had decided we were Fascists. The atmosphere was therefore very antagonistic. The interviewer, Magnus Magnusson, attacked us rather than interviewed us. To make matters worse, I was wearing dark clothes which, on television, made me look like a Blackshirt.

A rejection from the New York Film Festival was a cruel blow, losing us the chance of American interest. However, a showing at the London Film Festival was confirmed. At this stage the only distributor expressing interest was Tony Tenser, of Compton Films. Knowing the sort of films Compton specialised in, we were dismayed: we predicted their advertising campaign—'See the RAPE of a country! See a woman STRIPPED of her political ideals!!' But Tenser assured us that Compton would handle the film very carefully, and would allow us a say in the advertising. When we frankly confessed our opinion of Compton, Tenser was disarming. 'What can I say?' he said. 'It's like the man who offered a girl in a night club £5,000 to sleep with him. She accepted. Then he thought about it; £5,000... £500...'What about £50?' he asked. 'What do you think I am?' she replied. 'I thought we'd established that,' he said. 'Now we're working on a price.''

We postponed a decision until we had thoroughly investigated the matter. Woodfall encouraged us to accept. Tenser thought we would approach other distributors to compare offers, and gave warning that he would not become part of a Dutch auction. He sent us a letter demanding a decision within seven days.

The letter arrived, and the date expired while we were at the Cork Festival. Dick, Pauline, Andrew and I decided that *It Happened Here* had been almost worth the trouble, just to experience this splendid week. The Festival was Irish in every sense, except that it was uncharacteristically well organised. The film, miraculously, ceased to bother us—until we found that Frank Bennett had come, too.

The Irish had an odd habit of putting on the press conference before the film was shown and we had a hostile reception.

'What do you consider the main effect of occupation?' asked a journalist.

'Boredom and frustration,' replied Andrew, bluntly. 'Your freedom is restricted, there are curfews every night. The idea that everyone's in the resistance is absurd. Only a very small group in any country really resist.'

'Nonsense!' shouted someone from the audience.

The screening of the film was a damp squib after the fireworks of the press conference. Despite the Festival's fine organisation, the projection was erratic, and I spent the first reel running back and forth to the projection box, trying to get the picture in rack and in focus. The sound was too low and, as usual, it was muffled.

The public was plainly bored by it, but the Russian delegates invited it (unofficially) to the Moscow Film Festival, 'where it will get a big prize!' A German journalist said he had to go to bed after it and couldn't sleep at all: 'it was a nightmare'. But a lady journalist, reporting for a Scottish newspaper and the BBC, set a standard of disparagement seldom exceeded since: 'This film was made by two young men who are, I regret to say, British. Its hypothesis is inconceivable... it was shallow, immature and unfortunate... I could have enjoyed parts of it for laughs if I had not been writhing.'

However, one comment overshadowed all these. It came from the man who had shouted 'Nonsense!' at the press conference: Bert Haanstra, the great Dutch film-maker. A former Resistance worker, he knew the occupation intimately. He apologised for his remark, and told us how impressed he was. 'I thought I was back again, reliving the occupation,' he said. 'I got the impression that the Nazis in the film were real Nazis. Is this true?'

'It is.'

'But, surely, they don't exist any more?'

I introduced him to Frank Bennett, who promptly said: 'Don't you think we would solve the Jewish problem by sending all Jews to Madagascar?'

Haanstra was shaken. '*What* Jewish problem?' he asked. 'If there's a problem, it exists in your own mind.'

Our next Festival was Mannheim. This was my chance to visit Germany at long last. I was fascinated to see how different the Germans would be from the way we had portrayed them in the film. We crossed the border at midnight, and stopped at a *Gaststätte*. As we opened the door, right on cue, the rousing

181

strains of the marching song *Erika* came crashing from a juke-box...

The Festival was a complete contrast to Cork. Expecting a display of Teutonic efficiency, we were startled to see officials struggling with arrangements over tangled telephone wires, like signal troops in the bunker during the Fall of Berlin. The screening of the film was, again, disappointing and the projection was atrocious. Thirty members of the German Soldiers' Bund were among the audience; throughout the first half of the film, which is full of the atmosphere of occupation, the Germans responded well. They laughed at esoterica which only they would understand. But when the political discussion began, the atmosphere changed to one of smouldering hostility. Here, I thought, was the answer to those who thought the scene dangerous. The Germans were accustomed to war melodramas, which portrayed them as sadistic beasts. They could feel purged, knowing that they themselves were nothing like *that*. But the discussion scene was too near the knuckle. Here were Nazis talking just as *they* had talked, behaving just as they had behaved. It was too close for comfort.

At the end there were some isolated boos and some limp applause. North German Television interviewed some of the audience: 'Unfair to us Germans... disgusting that this film should be shown in Germany at this time...'

The press conference, held at 3.00 a.m., was crowded but hostile. There were few questions, but a great many statements. Delegates expressed their personal views on Nazism, the resistance, etc. Nobody talked about our film as a film; they discussed only its politics.

Several Frenchmen thought the film 'très dangereux'. One correspondent, an American Jew, was more outspoken. 'I salute you,' he said. 'You've done something here tonight that no one's done before. You've made these people think. I've been coming to this country every year since the end of the war and all I've ever met have been anti-Nazis. About time we realised what a heroic lot they must have been. You know, I'm still try-ing to work out how they face themselves in the shaving mirror each morning. They would like to think that your film can chip a little guilt from their black souls, but they know that that's not what it's really about.'

The only comment we heard from the jury was that the sound was bad.

Our next ordeal was the London Film Festival. We were as-signed a special screening at the Odeon, Leicester Square, at 11.00 a.m. on Sunday. This was a challenge, particularly as several members of the Festival staff warned us not to expect more than a few hundred people. If their publicity could attract no more than that, we would have to try. I wrote personal let-ters to every major film critic in London, enclosing a synopsis and background information. We had 2,066 seats to fill.

The press show, at the Odeon, Haymarket, was attended by more than two hundred people. The projection was impeccable; the focus was pin-sharp and the changeovers imperceptible. Furthermore, I was able to control the sound. I sat at the back of the theatre, and altered the volume of each sequence, restor-ing it to the level we had achieved in the dubbing theatre. I looked forward to the reviews.

The first I saw was in the *Telegraph*: it was headed WEAK STORY OF 'NAZI BRITAIN'. My heart sank as I read it. Eric Shorter had written the sort of review film-makers fear most: 'The result is totteringly implausible... an imaginative chal-lenge largely muffed. On the other hand, it is very much a fes-tival film and one which the London Film Festival has probably rescued from an undeserved obscurity. For although it is often naïve and shallow and technically weak and nowhere big enough for its subject, the heroism and ambition of such small-budget enterprises always deserves encouragement.'

The first sign of such encouragement appeared in the *Evening Standard*. Alexander Walker gave us the sort of notice that made our tribulations worthwhile: '...utterly absorbing entertainment... an eye-opener film, made with highly professional finish by a pair of assiduous amateurs, it vividly conjures up London under the SS... The weariness of defeat is almost tangible... Using several members of British Nazi groups, the script probes searchingly into the bad seeds of native Fascism.'

Thanks to this, and a number of other favourable reviews, we had a capacity crowd at the Odeon on Sunday morning. Several people were turned away, before the management permitted limited standing. The police stood by in case of incidents; Colin Jordan and a dozen members of the British National-Socialist Movement arrived to applaud Frank Bennett's pronouncements.

This was the one and only time that *It Happened Here* came over to our satisfaction. The projection at the Odeon, Leicester Square was as good as it had been at the Odeon, Haymarket, and once again I was able to control the sound. The large audience, which included many of our extras, understood the picture at once. The atmosphere was electric, and for the first time Andrew and I enjoyed what was usually an agonising experience. At the controversial discussion scene, the disbelieving laughter of the audience stifled the Colin Jordan group, who made no sound.

It was Sunday, 1 November 1964. The picture had taken only forty days to make, yet it was now eight years since our first session.

21: The Unkindest Cut

The *Jewish Chronicle* headed their review DEPLORABLE EFFORT, and described the film as an affront and an insult to the people of England.

'This thing is scrappy, ragged, uneven and slanted. No one will believe for a moment in the sheep-like acceptance of Hitlerian rule by the British people. They are made of sterner stuff than the milk-and-water people depicted here. It is deplorable that a considerable amount of footage is devoted to a dissertation of the National-Socialist credo against the Jews. The producers do not even allow one of the few anti-Nazi speaking characters to rebut this foul outpouring.'

Embassy Pictures' London representative strongly recommended the picture to his head office. Producer Leonard Lightstone rejected it without seeing it. 'I don't like the sound of the subject,' he explained. Columbia borrowed a print, and returned it with polite thanks a few weeks later, charging us for the cost of transportation to the U.S.A. The Board of Deputies of British Jews arranged a meeting with us to discuss the charges that the film was anti-Semitic. We were growing angry with this absurd label. 'Anyone who takes the mentally defective remarks of these Nazis at their face value must be as sick as they are,' I replied. 'How could we have someone putting the opposite point of view? The moment you argue with them, you accept their premise. You accept that people *can* be inferior because of their race. You may be able to accept this, we can't.'

The Board of Deputies agreed that most audiences would understand that the Nazis were self-condemnatory, 'but not all audiences are intelligent. Some may accept those words at their face value.'

'If they're that stupid, they'll be bored by the sequence,' I replied. The argument lasted two hours, during which we were warned that if the sequence remained, pressure might be brought to bear on our prospective distributors.

Nevertheless support for the film slowly grew. After our abortive encounter with the BFI's Experimental Film Fund, we were very touched by a letter from Stanley Reed: 'My warmest congratulations on the film, and no less on the way it has been received. I found it powerful and moving... I was anxious all the way through about the ending, as I could see no easy resolution. I thought your shocking final incident gave point to the whole picture and for me, at least, was the proper culmination of the film.'

Connoisseur Films offered us an excellent deal, which meant that we might open Academy Cinema Two. Tony Richardson had returned to England, however, and had screened the film to United Artists.

By sheer accident, I happened to be in United Artists' reception when a man announced he had been at a screening.

'One of ours?' asked someone.

'I hope not. I didn't like it. It was called *It Happened Here*.'

We were asked to meet the United Artists hierarchy a few days later. Among them was the man I had encountered the day before; he retained his deadpan, but there was a gleam of recognition in his eye. The UA executives said they liked the film, and were considering it for world-wide distribution. A month later, a contract was drawn up and our future looked bright. United Artists, the major distribution company in the world, had taken our film! It was too good to be true. Somehow, we never fully explained the position to Connoisseur, a discourtesy I shall always regret. Had we accepted their arrangement, and not been dazzled by the big name, our film would have been seen intact; we might even have made a little money out of it. The London editor of *Variety*, Harold Myers, warned us not to let the film go to a major company, but we foolishly refused to listen. 'You've got something very valuable there,' he said, 'provided it's properly exploited. If it goes to a major, it will be swallowed up.'

January 1965: Andrew formed the Historical Research Unit and left for Spain to act as technical adviser on *Dr Zhivago*. United Artists' legal department, under the terms of the contract, insisted on releases being signed by everyone in the cast. Some had emigrated, some had died, and tracing those we used in '57 and '58 required the resources of Pinkerton's. If only we had realised that this procedure might be necessary, it would have been a simple matter to pass out release forms during sessions.

We not only needed releases for appearances. One of the cast sued us for a photograph he had taken during our Parliament Square session, and which we had used for publicity. Had we secured his signature, we would have saved ourselves £550 costs and damages.

The question of whether the film would be cleared by the union—the Association of Cinematograph, Television and Allied Technicians—still had to be decided. If they blocked it, the chances of the film being seen in the British Isles were negligible. I talked to the General Secretary, George Elvin. Then we waited three suspense-filled months before a letter arrived informing us that the General Council had no objection relating to the film's distribution or exhibition. The decision, which had apparently run into opposition, was based on the fact that no union employees could have kept themselves available over such a long period.

'I must make it clear, however,' added George Elvin, 'that this is entirely without precedent and, in fact, arising out of the discussions on the matter the following resolution was carried by the General Council and will represent the Union's policy on future films of this kind: "That all future films made for any subject of propaganda comply with trade union practice and pay the rate if they are for public exhibition."'

The Observer scented a drama in my meeting with the

Board of Deputies of British Jews. John Ardagh came round for an interview. 'This affair is dead,' I said. 'For God's sake don't print anything or you'll start it up again.' He agreed to withhold the story for a while.

The catastrophe broke with the *Observer* of 9 May 1965: 'Leading Jewish circles... argue that the film's deadpan portrayals of Nazi propaganda and racial doctrines, intended as savagely ironic, might be taken literally by an unsophisticated audience and be dangerous.'

John Ardagh described how the film spent a year looking for a distributor, how people in the cinema world feared official Jewish and public reaction, and how it was finally taken up by United Artists. This was the first time the distributors' name had been made public. The article fanned the already smouldering fires of resentment. United Artists' publicity department was overwhelmed with telephone calls and deputations. A side-effect was a number of calls from people who had appeared in the film asking for money; they imagined that United Artists had paid us untold thousands for the rights: their advance, in fact, did not cover even the basic cost.

Alexander Walker countered with a broadside in our defence, in the *Evening Standard*. 'Like most people, I have never been a spectator at a Fascist rally. It was a revelation to me to be able to observe the dead calm manner, the smooth delivery and hear the insidious logic which the Fascists in the film use to brand a section of their fellow men as racial inferiors. To hear neo-Nazis thus condemn themselves out of their own mouths was far more effective than reading a dozen indictments of them by other people.'

Just as the controversy reached boiling point, I went to the Cannes Film Festival. The presentation of *It Happened Here* as part of the Critics Week clashed with the press show of William Wyler's *The Collector*. Outside, the beaches were sun-drenched. I realised, ruefully gazing at a half-empty house, that the place to hold a film festival is Manchester in March.

At the press conference, one man, who had fought with the FLN in Algeria, held the floor for almost half an hour. He was angered by our massacre sequence, and he accused the film of attacking the honour of the French resistance. At the conclusion of this lengthy outburst, another man rose to his feet. He said he had been in the resistance and that he had taken part in an action precisely the same as the one we had shown—'right down to the lorry'. The argument became heated, and I stood on the stage, pretending to understand it all while Louis Marcorelles, the organiser, whispered translations in my ear. At the end, an elderly Englishman stood up and said, simply, 'I just want to thank you for making it.' He walked out, and the press conference came to an end.

After the Festival, Woodfall called: did I know we had won the Semaine de la Critique award? Louis Marcorelles said there was no such thing. United Artists said that there was, and we had won it. Finally, the Federation of British Film Makers wrote to congratulate us on our *two* awards—the Critics Week Award and the Prize of the International Critics of Youth. We never received material proof of either.

25 October 1965: United Artists, who had still not released the picture, asked me to their office on a matter of importance. Was the picture at last to be given its West End showing? On the contrary, they said. It was going to be cut. The prime mover in this affair was the company's American President. The discussion scene offended him. Since he was standing as chairman of the National Finance Committee of the Democratic Party he could not ignore the protests from Jewish organisations. They warned him that if the film were shown complete, the repercussions would be enormous. Other executives at UA, I was told, opposed this cut, but their objections were overruled.

United Artists were morally committed to showing the film intact. But if we refused to cut the scene, then legal loopholes would be found in the contract.

I wrote to Wim van Leer in Israel, asking him if he would

intercede on our behalf. He wrote direct to the UA President, reminding him of his assistance with an Israeli documentary. He mentioned how impressed he had been with *It Happened Here*, and added: 'I have always felt that the best way to defeat subversion is by exposing it, basing myself on the general common sense of man who will evaluate it in the light of his own experience, and either accept it or reject it. The very outrageousness of the dialogue that takes place in the scene would only be taken amiss by a very sick mind. If you can accept my point, you would be promoting a beautiful filmic opportunity to expose the degrading idiocy of anti-Semitism.'

Andrew had returned from Spain and we talked over the dilemma. If we refused to let the sequence be cut, we risked the film disappearing; no other distributor would take it a year after its initial screening, and we had no guarantee that United Artists would give the film back to us. If we agreed to the cut, perhaps we could exert a little pressure of our own, and get the picture released at once.

Our strategy failed. 'The President took van Leer's letter in a very strange way,' we were told. 'It shook him. He did not feel he was wrong, but he admitted there were two sides to the question. He said that if Brownlow and Mollo felt that strongly, they would be welcome to set up with another distributor. If they agree to proceed with UA, we feel we are vulnerable. Therefore, we must ask for statements from both of you declaring that the cut was by mutual agreement.'

The picture had to be released. The discussion scene had been widely seen at Festivals. It would probably bore a general audience anyway. In this mood, we told UA to go ahead, although, luckily, we never had to sign those statements.

In December 1965 we were assured that the publicity campaign for the film would begin in three weeks. It did not.

In March 1966 United Artists told us that they planned to put the film on at the London Pavilion—after *Thunderball*. This James Bond picture was making huge sums, and 'After

Thunderball' sounded depressingly like After the Millennium.

A letter signed by Alexander Walker and ten other prominent critics appeared in *The Times*: 'To delete this sequence gravely damages the integrity of the film's argument, as well as its strength, and leaves it as simply another war film, although a bizarre and most imaginatively made one. Such censorship would also touch on the deeper question of democratic society—namely that of permitting all views to be heard however pernicious some of them will be to the majority. We consider this film is a responsible one in this respect and to censor it would betray a sad view of the public's intelligence and good sense.'

United Artists were incensed. 'What gets my goat,' said an executive, 'is that these critics think that one man is entitled to a personal opinion, but not one man who heads a multi-million dollar organisation.'

A letter signed by David Bickler, managing director of United Artists Corporation, appeared in *The Times* a few days later, and claimed that the presentation of the film reflected the mutual agreement of United Artists and the film's producers. 'It should be pointed out that revisions and refinements in the cut of a picture, at the option of the producer, are common practice in the film industry. It is the considered opinion of both the distributors and the producers that the slight deletion referred to in no way affects the continuity or the integrity of the story.'

The controversy continued. Meanwhile, David Bickler endeavoured to find a solid supporting film for *It Happened Here*. He admitted that he thought the picture would die a lamentable death if it was shown on its own. 'What about *The Knack*?' he asked.

'No,' I said. 'That would be a re-run. Let's have the film on its own, with a short or a second feature.'

A few weeks later, David Bickler suggested *The War Game*, Peter Watkins' film which had been banned by the BBC. Since

(Left) the London Pavilion, May 1966, and (right) advertising for a Soviet documentary at the Cameo-Royal, July 1966

our film was about England losing the last war, and Peter's was about England losing the next one, I asked UA to take pity on the poor audiences.

'Let's face facts,' said David Bickler. 'We're all in this business to make money. Now, we don't mind putting your film on at the Pavilion. We don't mind losing £2,000 a week and taking it off after a fortnight. But I'm thinking of you. I'd like to see you make a little money.' But we wanted *It Happened Here* to stand on its own, and David Bickler finally agreed to show it with a second feature. 11 May 1966: the most satisfying sight I can remember. The *Thunderball* display being removed from the front of the London Pavilion, and being replaced with a huge picture of German troops marching past Big Ben and, in large red letters, IT HAPPENED HERE—the story of the German occupation of England.

As the London Film Festival screening had been the climax of our years of struggle, so this represented our victory in the search for a distributor. In the first weeks our takings rivalled *The Knack* and *Tom Jones*. There were queues every night. The critics gave us unanimously good notices. United Artists were delighted. 'How does it feel to be rich?' they asked.

The London Pavilion, May 1966

The film booked in to follow ours was moved to the Plaza and *Alfie* came off instead. UA took a full page in the trade press showing a picture of the Pavilion and part of a queue: THIS BUSINESS HAPPENS HERE EVERY DAY!

Distributors began to phone up, asking us whether the overseas rights had been sold. They had. 'May I point out,' I said to Rank, 'that you are just two years too late?'

'That wouldn't have happened,' said the Rank man hastily, 'if *I'd* been with the firm then.'

The takings fluctuated with the weather. I kept a careful check on the standard of projection.

Prince Marshall took some friends to an evening show, and the titles came on out of focus. He left his seat, and asked an usherette to call up the projectionists on the house phone.

'It's the print, dear,' she said. 'We can't do a thing about it.'

Our figures were knocked down by a heat-wave, which affected the whole of the West End although we remained among the major money-makers. At the end of six weeks UA decided to transfer it to another West End cinema—the Prince Charles. David Bickler said that he had found an ideal support: *Camp on Blood Island.* 'Frankly, we consider that the programme will

193

take off. I admit I under-estimated the money-making potential of your film. Nevertheless, it needs a little support for release.'

'I don't question that,' I said. 'But please don't put those two together.'

'The type of person who would go to see your film, would go to see *Camp on Blood Island*—the swastika and the Rising Sun, as it were.'

'The type of person who would want to see Camp on Blood Island would be someone who derives enjoyment from sadism.'

'If you feel like that, we won't transfer,' said David Bickler crossly.

He called me the next day and said, with a laugh, that we would never see eye to eye, but that he had transferred the original programme to the Gala Royal. The picture lasted three weeks there and then it mysteriously vanished from London. It was shown in various parts of England, but a circuit release, it was clear, was not to be granted.

When I called the man in charge of circuit bookings at Rank, he lost his temper as soon as he realised who I was. 'How dare you telephone me direct? Who do you think you are? Do you think Otto Preminger rings up to find out why we didn't give his film a circuit booking?'

Although the film made £23,000* at its Pavilion run, the money, we were told, was completely absorbed by distribution and advertising costs. The film was shown in New York, Los Angeles, Paris, Stockholm, Copenhagen, Haifa and elsewhere with very favourable press reaction. Nevertheless, we made no money. On the official returns, promotion costs swallowed up our profits. *It Happened Here* had a final negative cost of £7,000*. The trailers for the picture, lasting three minutes but produced professionally, cost $4,298*. Our eight years of pro-

*Correcting approximately for inflation from 1966 to 2005 using the Retail Price Index, £23,000 would become £131,000, £7,000 would become £39,900 and $4,298 would become $24,500.

duction netted us not one penny.

A distributor is very much of a mixed blessing. You cannot secure a public showing without one, but the moment he takes your film, you lose control over it. Understandably, he will never feel as strongly about it as you, nor will he fight for it as energetically. Our distributors accepted Rank and ABC's rejection without argument, something we would never have done. They had far too many pictures to worry about and many more thousands at stake.

The situation was no brighter behind the Iron Curtain. *It Happened Here* was unanimously accepted by the committee which selects foreign films for exhibition in the U.S.S.R., and unanimously rejected by the committee of cinema managers. They regarded it as 'non-commercial'.

Fortunately we did not make *It Happened Here* for money. We made it because we had to. It gave us an apprentice course in the problems of film production. Whatever its financial and artistic shortcomings, the experience has been endlessly rewarding.

There is an ironic postscript. After *It Happened Here*, we tried to set up a new feature, to be made within the industry. Each idea was greeted with the reaction we knew so well—'it's just not commercial'. But there was a subtle difference. This time the producers said: 'Now if you had come along with an idea like your last one—with *that* kind of impact—why, we'd be right behind you.'

196

Checklist: Kevin Brownlow

Born 2 June 1938, Crowborough, Sussex

Film Work

1955 *The Capture*   (UK; 9.5mm amateur film) Director

1958 *Band Wagon*   (UK; d. Peter Hopkinson) Editor/ Co-scriptwriter with John Krish

1961 *Ascot, a Race against Time* (UK) Director, Editor

1962 *Nine, Dalmuir West* (UK) Director, Photography, Editor, Narration written by

1963 *Francis Bacon: Paintings* 1944—1962 (UK; d. David Thompson) Editor

1964 *It Happened Here* (UK) Co-director, Producer, Screenplay with Andrew Mollo; Additional Photography (16mm), Editor

I Think They Call Him John (UK; d. John Krish) Editor

Parade   (UK; d. Derek Hill) Photography

1966 *Turkey - The Bridge* (UK; d. Derek Williams) Editor

1967 *Red and Blue*   (UK; d. Tony Richardson) Editor

The White Bus   (UK; d. Lindsay Anderson) Editor

1968 *The Charge of the Light Brigade* (UK; d. Tony Richardson) Supervising Editor

Millay at Steepletop Director, Photography, Editor

1975 *Winstanley*   (UK) Co-director, Producer with Andrew Mollo

No Surrender   (UK/Canada; d. Peter Smith) Supervising Editor

(Plus numerous industrial and sponsored films, for Unilever, Wimpey, Handley-Page, COI etc.)

Television Work

1966 *Crisis on Wheels* (UK; ATV) Director
1968 *Omnibus: Abel Gance - The Charm of Dynamite*
(UK; BBC) Director, Script, Editor
1980 *Hollywood* (UK; series Thames TV, 13 eps) Co-director, Producer, Script with David Gill
1983 *Unknown Chaplin* (UK; series; Thames TV, 3 eps) Co-director, Producer, Script with David Gill
1986 *British Cinema Personal View* (UK; series, Thames TV: 3 eps) Series Producers: David Gill and KB
Buster Keaton - A Hard Act to Follow (UK/US; series; Thames TV, 3 eps 1987) Co-director, Producer, Script with David Gill
1990 *Harold Lloyd: The Third Genius* UK/US; series; Thames TV, 2 eps) Co-director, Producer, Scrip with David Gill
1993 *D.W. Griffith: Father of Film* (US/UK; 3 eps) Co-director, Producer, Script with David Gill
1995 *Cinema Europe: The Other Hollywood* (UK/France/Germany; series, 6 eps) Co- director, Producer, Script with David Gill
1998 *Universal Horror* (US,UK; Director, Editor)
2000 *Lon Chaney - A Thousand Faces* (UK/US) Director, Editor

2002 The Tramp and the Dictator (UK/Germany) Co-
Director with Michael Kloft,
Narration written by
2004 *Cecil B. De Mille - American Epic* (US) Director
2004 *So Funny It Hurt: Buster Keaton and MGM*
Co-director with Christopher Bird
2005 (in production) *Greta Garbo; Merian C. Cooper*

Restoration Work   Over 25 films including:

Ben-Hur A Tale of the Christ (d. Fred Niblo, 1925)
The Eagle (d. Clarence Brown, 1925)
Napoléon (d. Abel Gance, 1927)
The Thief of Bagdad (d. Raoul Walsh, 1924)
The Crowd (d. King Vidor, 1928)
The Wind (d. Victor Sjöström, 1928)
The Four Horsemen of the Apocalypse (d. Rex Ingram, 1921)
The Iron Horse (d. John Ford, 1924)
Sunrise (d. F.W. Murnau, 1927)
The Phantom of the Opera (d. Rupert Julian, 1925)
The Wedding March (d. Erich von Stroheim, 1928)
The Iron Mask (d. Allan Dwan, 1929)
The Cat and the Canary (d. Paul Leni, 1927)
Sherlock Holmes (d. Al Parker, 1922)
Show People (d. King Vidor, 1928)

Books

How It Happened Here (1968)
The Parade's Gone by ... (1968)
Hollywood: The Pioneers (1979)
The War, the West and the Wilderness (1979)

Napoleon, Abel Gance's Classic Film (1983)
Behind the Mask of Innocence (1990)
David Lean: A Biography (1996)
Mary Pickford Rediscovered (1999)

Checklist: Andrew Mollo

Andrew Mollo was born in Epsom, Surrey, on 15 May 1940. His father was half Russian and his mother English. The family lived in Farnham, Surrey, and moved to London in 1956 when Andrew was sixteen. While studying sculpture at the Regent Street Polytechnic Kevin Brownlow enlisted his help with his amateur film *It Happened Here*. In 1960, on his return from studying in Paris, he worked as Harry Saltzman's 'tea-boy' on *Saturday Night and Sunday Morning*. Staying with Woodfall Films, Andrew worked as assistant director on *A Taste of Honey* and *Loneliness of the Long Distance Runner*. From the mid-1960's to the mid-1970's he worked as Technical Adviser on such films as *Dr.Zhivago*, *Night of the Generals* and *The Keep*. In 1975 Kevin Brownlow and Andrew Mollo completed their second feature film *Winstanley* which was financed by the British Film Institute. In 1980—quite by chance—Andrew started a new career as Production Designer on feature films and television. He designed all fourteen episodes of *Sharpe* for Carlton and the first two episodes of *Hornblower*. Since being nominated for a prime-time Emmy for *The Even Chance*, he has reverted to consulting on films about World War 2 and the Holocaust. Andrew now lives in central France and has spent the last two years working in Germany.

Credits as Co-Director, Features

Year	Title	Company	Co-Directors
1975	*Wnstanley*	BFI	Kevin Brownlow Andrew Mollo
1965	*It Happened Here*	UA	Kevin Brownlow Andrew Mollo

Selected credits as Military/Historical Advisor

Year	Title	Company	Director
2004	*Die Letzte Schlacht*	Cinecentrum	C.Blumenberg
2004	*Speer und Er*	Bavaria	H.Breleur
2003	*Der Untergang* (Downfall)	Konstantin	O.Hirschbiegel
2002	*The Origins of Evil*	CBS	C. Duguay
2001	*A Lonely War*	Labrador	R.Loncraine
2001	*The Pianist*	R.P.Prods	R.Polanski
2000	*Conspiracy-Meeting at Wansee*		Frank Pierson
2000	*The Grey Zone*	Killer	T.Blake-Nelson
1982	*The Keep*	Paramount	Michael Mann
1967	*The Dirty Dozen*	MGM/UA	John Sturges
1966	*The Night of the Generals*	Horizon	Anatole Litvak
1966	*Roi du Coeur*		P.de Broca
1965	*Doctor Zhivago*	MGM	David Lean

Selected credits as Production Designer (TV)

Year	Title	Company	Director
1997	*Hornblower* (1st 2 episodes*)	Meridian	Andrew Grieve
1993-6	*Sharpe* (all 14 episodes)	Central	Tom Clegg

Selected credits as Production Designer (Features)

Year	Title	Company	Director
1987	*Pascali's Island*	Working Title	James Dearden
1985	*No Surrender*	Palace Pictures	Peter Smith
1984	*Dance with a Stranger*		Mike Newell
1982	*Xtro*	Amalgamated	H. Bromley-Davenport

Selected credits as Director/Writer (Documentaries)

Year	Title	Company	Director
1980	*The History of the SS*	Thames TV	
	La Bataille de Naseby	Pathe	H.de Turenne
	Jordanian Armed Forces	Jordan TV	A.Balfour-Fraser

*First episode (*Even Chance*) nominated for Primetime Emmy for Best Production Design. Further biographical information on Internet Movie Database: http://imdb.com/

Afterword: The View from Forty Years On

As soon as the film was in distribution, I began to travel around Europe with it. (Andrew was working on other films.) It opened in Paris, appropriately at the *Cinema Napoléon*, as *En Angleterre Occupé*. It brought me into contact with Bernard Eisenschitz, who made no secret of the fact that he disliked the film. But we liked each other and have stayed friends for forty years. The Swedish release enabled me to meet the enchanting silent actress Karin Molander, widow of Lars Hanson. United Artists were not generous enough to fly me to the United States, but the film opened at the Little Carnegie cinema in New York to reviews in *Time* and *Newsweek* which made me think we'd arrived. But it did not do the business UA had hoped.

A friend from World Wide, Peter Hopkinson, showed the film in India and afterwards a woman came to commiserate with him on the sufferings of England under the Nazis. She was convinced it had actually happened. (Peter Hopkinson was subsequently instrumental in getting this book published.)

We began to think of our next project. We naively expected that those who ran the picture business would be only too glad to finance two young film-makers who had proved their ability by writing, producing and directing a 99-minute feature film for only £7,000.

But we rapidly learned that the film industry does not welcome such idiosyncrasy. Had we spent seven million, we should have been warmly embraced, for we would be a conduit to the source of the money. And in the surreal world of film finance, a producer who sets out to make a film for very little and succeeds is far less significant than one who wildly overspends. The first is forgotten. The second is the producer of a multi-million dollar production.

205

Besides which, our picture had proved controversial. The word went around the industry that it was 'anti-Semitic.' Andrew and I were invited to meet many producers, but no project ever resulted.

I have since learned that once a film begins to lose money, it is in the distributors' interest to heap all sorts of other costs on to it. The former head of UA in London, George Ornstein commiserated with us. We had, apparently, been given a very raw deal. No one knew it better than he. When he left UA to join Harry Saltzman making the Bond films, he had set up a group of accountants to check UA's figures. On their first survey, they compared the returns from Tokyo with the exchange rate of the yen and found that UA had been $56,000 short. The yen had been exchanged when the rates were favourable to the Americans, but this fact had been concealed.

UA's returns came in steadily, showing tremendous losses from screenings in all parts of the world. I sometimes received reviews from friends in outlying places, but those places never appeared on the returns. UA had the nerve to ask for their advance back. With the losses allegedly reaching the staggering figure of $127,000, they evidently decided to save postage and the returns stopped arriving.

We thought we should commemorate the mournful occasion with a *Gala Derniere* at the Tolmer, Tottenham Court Road (a fleapit in which all seats were 9d.) for the benefit of our creditors in the absence of H M the Queen. (Black armbands.)

We worked on a project about the Norman invasion, based on a novel called *The Golden Warrior* with the blessing of its author, Hope Muntz. We decided we needed a professional scriptwriter, but he, in cahoots with our agent, decided that Universal would pay more and sold it to them without a word to us. It was never made, but we learned a lot about the industry in this fallow period.

We thought the novel *The Breaking of Bumbo* would, for

once, be a reasonably commercial project. We hammered away at a script for Philip Mackie at Granada Films, until he decided the script was no good and fired us. The project was taken up by the novel's author, Andrew Sinclair. He wrote a script and had it accepted by Bryan Forbes at Associated British Picture Corporation. Forbes agreed that Andrew and I could direct. We were to be part of his revitalisation of the British Film Industry. It was exhilarating to be about to embark on our first professional feature. But aspects of the script worried me, and the casting even more so. We suddenly lost our leading man and discovered the producer, an American, had been duplicitous. We foolishly challenged him. We were off the picture immediately.

The best part of the experience was when Andrew and I attended an upper-class wedding to get background for the film and he introduced me to a red-headed Irish girl, Virginia Keane. We married in 1969.

With Virginia, I went off to work for the American Film Institute in California. A few years earlier, Andrew and I had written a script based on a historical novel called *Comrade Jacob*, by David Caute, which Miles Halliwell had brought to our attention. It was set just after the Civil War and dealt with a group of what would now be called Christian Communists known as The Diggers. We fell in love with it and Woodfall gave us the money to develop the script. But no one wanted to finance it. We had some hilarious rejections. My favourite was the American producer who said 'I've read your script. I think it's great.' (They always say that.) 'But I just don't like Winstanley. Now, I don't think you have to like the leading man. Genghiz Khan in Henry Levin's picture wasn't exactly likeable. But he had a fine relationship with a girl.' So I had no great hope of ever making it, when Mamoun Hassan became head of the British Film Institute Production Board. He put the idea up to the board and it was accepted. He sent me a telegram in 1972: COME HOME. YOUR PROBLEMS ARE JUST

207

BEGINNING.

We made *Winstanley*—with Miles Halliwell playing the lead—very much as we had made IHH. In 1976, we celebrated twenty years of working together—with only two films under our belts, and both made outside the industry.

I had only one 35mm print of IHH, and I loaned it to the Other Cinema to be shown when they premiered *Winstanley*. When it failed to come back, I telephoned the Other Cinema and they explained that weeks before they had put it in a taxi. The address? 'Oh, 13 Queen's Gate.' I lived in 13 Queens Gate Place. So I went round to see if it was still sitting in a hallway.

'Yes, there was a film,' I was told. 'A taxi driver dumped it on our steps. When no one picked it up we called the police. The policeman examined a roll and the middle fell out. He put it back in the can and when it didn't fit he just banged the lid back until it did.' I recovered the print from the police station, and did what I could to repair the damaged sections.

Around this period, I began to investigate ways of getting the rights for IHH back from United Artists. First, an executive of UA, David Picker, wanted me to serve on the board of one of his committees, and I agreed, provided he arranged for me to get the rights back. No dice.

In 1976, Stanley Kubrick put his lawyer on to trying to find a way to recover the rights, because it was a film he considered worth reviving. But even he met with stalemate.

The reaction to *Winstanley* in the UK made me realise that no feature offers were liable to result.

When my restoration of Abel Gance's *Napoléon* was a smash hit in New York, in 1981, the head of United Artists rang me at my hotel to say how impressed he had been. I raised the questions of the IHH rights, and he said, bluntly, 'We never give our rights back.' I happened to know, I said, that they had made an exception with Francois Truffaut. But there was to be no exception for me.

It took years and years, but eventually, in the 1990s, I

heard that Lindsay Doran had become President of UA. I knew her from my time in California, and I liked her very much. I told her of the background, and in a very short time she had arranged with the lawyers, who must have been apoplectic, for me to have the rights for my lifetime. Motion picture lawyers would far prefer to incinerate a film rather than return it to its director. As it was, it had taken thirty years. But it proves the old adage that it isn't what you know that counts in this business, but who you know.

The video revolution gave the film a new lease of life. Once I got the rights, it was possible to bring the film out on video. The British Film Institute distributed it in the UK but only on VHS. Rather more enterprising, in the USA, Dennis Doros of Milestone Films not only brought it out on video and eventually DVD, but he reissued the film theatrically in a double bill with *Winstanley*. Doros sent the reviews. I wish we had got such glowing reactions when the film first appeared!

I took the film to some intriguing venues. In the Channel Islands, where I thought it would be understood as nowhere else, it was deeply unpopular and the Q & A session after the show revealed that some members of the audience took it as a direct criticism of their behaviour during the war and as such, they regarded it as an insult.

Pauline Jobson, the doctor's wife from New Radnor, Powys, Wales, who played the lead, died of cancer in 1994. She never had another part in a film, but the experience gave her the confidence to direct the plays the local WI put on in New Radnor. Dr Richard Jobson, her husband, had died a few years earlier. All of us remained in close contact and Jo and Peter Suschitzky bought a cottage nearby. Peter had meanwhile become a Hollywood cameraman, with films like *The Empire Strikes Back* to his credit.

I was not interested in working in television. I was so snobbish about it I did not even own a set. The one programme I was obsessed by was The World at War, and Virginia and I had to go to see it at the flat of Ian Sellar, an old comrade from *Winstanley*, and his wife Linda. She hated anything to do with warfare and used to lie on the divan with her back to the set. When the series was repeated, I bought a TV.

I wrote a fan letter to the producer, Jeremy Isaacs, and in his reply he told me of an extraordinary coincidence. As a farewell present to his crew, he had given them a copy of my book on silent films *The Parade's Gone By...*. He thought there might be a series in it. Would I like to work on it? Well, actually no. I thought going into television would act like an alcoholic's cure. It would end my enthusiasm for silent films. Virginia forced me into it. Jeremy Isaacs turned out to be an enlightened producer, and while I was at first just writer and consultant, I was given a partner, David Gill, and we became director-producers for the next four years. The result was a thirteen part series called *Hollywood* (1980). Since then, I have specialised in documentaries on film history.

In the 1990s, a Hollywood screenwriter tried to take an option on our script for *It Happened Here* in order to remake it. But United Artists insisted they had retained the remake rights, and now that Lindsay Doran had left, the lawyers rapidly brought about the collapse of the whole project.

I remember when I first began to shoot the film, in 1956, I thought: 'It's eleven years after the war. No one will be interested!' Sixty years after the war, hardly an evening goes by without a documentary on Hitler on television, and Andrew Mollo has just worked as technical adviser on a number of feature films about World War II, including Roman Polanski's *The Pianist*. I only wish we could have made a few of them together.

K.B.   London   2005

Acknowledgements

Thanks are due to the following for permission to include in this book photographs taken by them: Rosemary Claxton, Brewster Cross, Aubrey Dewar, Robert Freeman, Pat Kearney, London News Agency, Prince Marshall, Chris Menges, Derek Milburn, Eric Mival, Andrew Mollo, P.G. Pearce-Smith, Graham Samuel, Peter Suschitzky, Pat Sullivan, and Peter Watkins. All other pictures are from Kevin Brownlow's collection.

Lightning Source UK Ltd.
Milton Keynes UK
UKOW052123270212

188031UK00001B/135/A